THE TARE ANRD THE S IMBKAR

INDIAN MYTHOLOGY

FICTION BECOMING FACTS

THE ENCISTTING DRLESAMGNY TN REILSTOS

PRAKHAR MISHRA

DOLEBDTION MEI MACUAR Y HW LIGADEN

Unveil the Timeless Secrets of Indian Mythology in "Indian Mythology: Fiction Becoming Facts" by Prakhar Mishra.

Step into a realm where ancient myths burst into the realm of reality. In this provocative exploration, Prakhar Mishra harnesses groundbreaking research to transform what we thought were mere fables into historical truths. This book is not just an educational journey—it's an invitation to debate and rediscover the global resonance of Indian mythology.

With each chapter, "Indian Mythology: Fiction Becoming Facts" challenges preconceptions, unveiling how these age-old stories transcend time and geography to influence contemporary life and culture worldwide. Aimed at curious minds aged 20 to 70, this book beckons you to question the boundaries between history and mythology.

Prepare to be enthralled as you connect with powerful deities, epic battles, and divine prophecies that are proving to be as factual as they are inspirational. Whether you're a devoted mythologist or a skeptical historian, this book will ignite discussions, spark controversies, and inspire a newfound appreciation for the myths that have shaped civilizations.Embrace the debate and delve into a world where fiction and fact converge—your view of history will never be the same again.

Indian Mythology

Fiction Becoming Facts

PRAKHAR MISHRA

Dated: 24/04/2024

Publisher's Name:- Prakhar Mishra
Publisher's Address:- 12/107, Vikas Nagar, Lucknow, Uttar Pradesh - 226022
Email Address:- prakharm761@gmail.com

First Edition

Acknowledgements

I would like to express my deepest gratitude to my family and friends for their unwavering support and encouragement throughout the journey of writing this book. Their patience and understanding have been a constant source of strength for me, and this work would not have been possible without their love and encouragement.

A special thank you to my parents: ***Mr. Raj Narayan Mishra and Mrs. Sandhya Mishra*** and my wife, ***Priyanshi*** whose endless love and guidance have always inspired me to pursue my passions. Their wisdom and teachings have been the bedrock of my personal and professional life.

To my friends, who have provided invaluable feedback and insightful discussions that helped refine my thoughts and ideas presented in this work. Your perspectives and critiques have been immensely helpful in shaping this book.

I am also grateful to all those who contributed indirectly to my journey, whose stories and experiences have enriched my understanding of the vast and complex tapestry of Indian mythology.

Lastly, I extend my thanks to everyone who has been a part of this journey, for it is your collective belief in my abilities that has allowed me to turn my vision into reality.

Contents

Introduction (Page 10-11)

Chapter 1: The Role of Mythology in Indian Literature:

- The Significance of Mythological Characters (**Page 12-18**)
- The Influence of Mythology on Themes and Plot of Indian Movies (**Page 19-27**)
- The Use of Mythological Symbols and Motifs (**Page 28-35**)
- Key Myths and stories (**Page 36-47**)

Chapter 2: Ancient Indian Epics: The Foundation of Mythological Literature

- The Ramayana: A Tale of Virtue and Duty (**Page 48-64**)
- The Mahabharata: The Battle of Good and Evil (**Page 65-82**)

- The Puranas: Cosmic Tales of Creation and Destruction (**Page 83-98**)

Chapter 3: The Impact of Indian Mythology in Contemporary Literature

- Novels, Short Stories and Contemporary Literature Inspired by Mythology, Mythological Retellings and Adaptations (**Page 99-122**)
- The Tales of Panchatantra: Lessons in Morality and their Impact (**Page 123-139**)
- Mythological Folk Songs and Poetry, The Use of Gods and Goddesses as Literary Symbols (**Page 140-156**)

Chapter 4: Historical and Archaeological Evidence - *DWARKA, AYODHYA, MAHABHARATA & THE RAM-SETU*

- Exploration of archaeological findings supporting mythological events (**Page 157-174**)
- Historical records corroborating mythological narratives (**Page 175-188**)

Chapter 5: Scientific Interpretations

- Examination of scientific theories aligning with mythological accounts (**Page 189-201**)
- Examples of how modern science explains mythical phenomena (**Page 202-210**)

Chapter 6: Controversies and Debates

- Addressing controversies surrounding interpretations of Indian mythology (**Page 211-229**)

Conclusion: Reflection on the enduring relevance of Indian mythology (Page 230-236)

THANK YOU NOTE (Page 237-238)

INTRODUCTION

Indian mythology is a tapestry woven with threads of gods, goddesses, heroes, and mythical creatures, spanning millennia of human imagination and storytelling. What began as oral traditions passed down through generations evolved into intricate epics and sacred texts that continue to captivate minds around the world.

In the vast landscape of Indian mythology, there exists a fascinating phenomenon where fiction intersects with reality, blurring the lines between what is imagined and what is believed to be true. This e-book delves into the enigmatic realm where ancient myths and legends transform into tangible historical events, supported by archaeological discoveries, scientific interpretations, and cultural influences.

Join us on a journey through the corridors of time as we explore the rich tapestry of Indian mythology, unraveling the mysteries that lie beneath the surface and discovering how the fantastical narratives of the past continue to shape our understanding of the world today.

Chapter 1: The Role of Mythology in Indian Literature

The Significance of Mythological Characters:

Mythological characters hold a revered status in Indian literature, serving as timeless archetypes that embody the essence of human experience and the eternal struggle between good and evil.

These characters, drawn from ancient epics, Puranas (ancient texts), and folk tales, transcend the boundaries of time and space, resonating with readers across generations. Here, we delve into the profound significance of mythological characters and their enduring impact on Indian literature.

1. Archetypal Representations:

Mythological characters in Indian literature serve as archetypal representations of fundamental human traits, virtues, and vices. Whether it's the righteous and noble hero like Rama from the Ramayana or the cunning and complex anti-hero like Krishna from the Mahabharata, these characters embody universal qualities that mirror the complexities of human nature. Through their actions, struggles, and triumphs, they offer profound insights into the human condition, providing readers with timeless lessons and moral guidance.

2. Cultural and Religious Significance:

Mythological characters are deeply embedded in the cultural and religious fabric of India, revered as divine beings and sources of spiritual wisdom. For millions of Hindus, characters like Vishnu, Shiva, Lakshmi, Durga, and Hanuman are not just mythical figures but objects of devotion and worship. Their stories, rituals, and symbolism permeate every aspect of Indian life, from daily prayers and festivals to art, music, and literature. In Indian literature, these characters serve as embodiments of divine grace, power, and wisdom, inspiring awe and reverence in readers.

3. Narrative Complexity and Depth:

The richness and complexity of Indian mythology are reflected in the multifaceted nature of its characters. Mythological literature presents a diverse array of characters, each with their own strengths, weaknesses, and moral dilemmas. Whether it's the epic hero struggling to uphold dharma (righteousness) like Arjuna in the Mahabharata or the conflicted goddess torn between love and duty like Sita in the Ramayana, these characters navigate intricate webs of relationships, emotions, and ethical dilemmas, offering readers a glimpse into the complexities of human existence.

4. Evolution and Adaptation:

One of the remarkable aspects of mythological characters is their ability to evolve and adapt over time, reflecting the changing aspirations, values, and concerns of society. From ancient oral traditions to classical texts and contemporary literature, mythological characters have undergone countless reinterpretations and adaptations, resonating with each generation in new and unexpected ways. Writers and poets continue to draw inspiration from these characters, reimagining them in diverse settings and contexts, from modern urban landscapes to futuristic dystopias, keeping their timeless essence alive in the ever-changing tapestry of Indian literature.

5. Symbolism and Allegory:

Mythological characters in Indian literature often serve as symbols and allegories, representing abstract concepts, philosophical ideas, and moral principles. Whether it's the metaphorical journey of the hero through the trials and tribulations of life or the symbolic battle between light and darkness, these characters offer layers of meaning that extend beyond the literal narrative. Through their symbolic significance, mythological characters invite readers to contemplate profound truths and existential questions, transcending the boundaries of time and space to explore the depths of human consciousness.

In conclusion, mythological characters in Indian literature are more than mere figures of myth and legend; they are embodiments of timeless truths, cultural symbols, and spiritual archetypes that continue to inspire, enlighten, and captivate readers across the ages. Through their narratives, these characters offer profound insights into the human condition, inviting readers to embark on a journey of self-discovery, moral reflection, and spiritual awakening.

This section has explored the multifaceted significance of mythological characters in Indian literature, highlighting their archetypal nature, cultural significance, narrative complexity, evolution, and symbolic depth. Through their enduring presence in the literary landscape, mythological characters continue to weave the threads of myth and legend into the rich tapestry of Indian storytelling, enchanting readers with their timeless wisdom and eternal relevance.

xxx~¬~xxx

The Influence of Mythology on Themes and Plot of Indian Movies:

Indian cinema, with its vibrant tapestry of storytelling traditions, draws deeply from the wellspring of mythology to craft narratives that resonate with audiences across the subcontinent and beyond. Mythological themes, characters, and motifs permeate Indian movies, infusing them with a timeless quality and a profound cultural resonance. In this exploration, we delve into the multifaceted influence of mythology on the themes and plotlines of Indian cinema, examining how ancient epics and legends continue to inspire and enrich contemporary storytelling.

1. Battle Between Good and Evil:

One of the most enduring themes drawn from mythology is the epic battle between good and evil. Indian movies often depict this timeless struggle, portraying noble heroes and virtuous heroines pitted against formidable villains and malevolent forces. Drawing inspiration from mythological epics such as the Ramayana and the Mahabharata, these movies explore the triumph of righteousness over tyranny, the victory of light over darkness. Whether it's the righteous valor of Rama in "Ramayana: The Legend of Prince Rama" or the epic clash between Pandavas and Kauravas in "Mahabharat," Indian cinema celebrates the eternal struggle between dharma (righteousness) and adharma (lawlessness).

2. Quest for Identity and Destiny:

Mythological narratives often revolve around the quest for identity, purpose, and destiny, themes that resonate deeply with Indian cinema. Characters embark on transformative journeys of self-discovery, grappling with questions of heritage, lineage, and destiny. From the epic odyssey of Arjuna in "Arjun: The Warrior Prince" to the mythic quest of Shiva in "Devon Ke Dev... Mahadev," Indian movies explore the timeless quest for self-realization and enlightenment, drawing inspiration from ancient myths and legends that speak to the human condition.

3. Love, Devotion, and Sacrifice:

Love, devotion, and sacrifice are central themes in Indian mythology, finding expression in the romantic sagas of gods and goddesses, as well as the enduring bonds of friendship and familial duty. Indian movies often weave these themes into their narratives, portraying epic love stories, divine romances, and selfless acts of sacrifice. Whether it's the eternal love of Radha and Krishna in "Krishna Leela" or the self-sacrifice of Sita in "Sita Sings the Blues," Indian cinema celebrates the transformative power of love and devotion, echoing the timeless tales of mythology.

4. Moral Dilemmas and Ethical Choices:

Mythological tales are replete with moral dilemmas and ethical choices that test the characters' virtues and principles. Indian movies explore these themes, presenting characters grappling with complex moral quandaries and ethical decisions. Whether it's the moral dilemma faced by Arjuna on the battlefield of Kurukshetra in "Mahabharat" or the ethical choices confronting Rama in "Sri Ramadutham Hanuman," Indian cinema invites viewers to ponder the timeless questions of right and wrong, duty and loyalty, honor and integrity, echoing the moral complexities of ancient myths and legends.

5. Redemption and Transformation:

Redemption and transformation are recurring motifs in Indian mythology, as characters undergo profound journeys of spiritual growth and enlightenment. Indian movies often depict these themes, portraying characters who undergo inner transformation and find redemption through trials and tribulations. Whether it's the spiritual awakening of Prince Siddhartha in "Buddha: The Great Departure" or the redemption of the fallen warrior Karna in "Karna," Indian cinema celebrates the power of redemption and the possibility of personal transformation, drawing inspiration from the timeless tales of mythology.

Thematic Incorporations in Cinema:

- **"Brahmastra":** This is an Indian fantasy film that, engages with concepts of ancient weapons and mythological elements in a contemporary setting. The title "Brahmastra" refers to a mythical weapon described in ancient texts, which could be seen as an extension of the grand cosmic narratives and powers like those in the Hiranyagarbha story.

- **"Baahubali" Series (2015, 2017):** These films, directed by S.S. Rajamouli, capture the essence of mythical storytelling, creation, and epic narratives reminiscent of the grandeur and philosophical depth seen in stories like Hiranyagarbha. The tale of birth, royal lineage, and the protagonist's journey closely aligns with the cyclic themes of cosmic and personal renewal and destruction.

- **"Magadheera" (2009):** Directed by S.S. Rajamouli, this film explores themes of reincarnation and eternal love, echoing the cyclic nature of creation and destruction inherent in the Hiranyagarbha concept. The story revolves around lovers reincarnated to fulfill their love in another life, symbolizing renewal and continuation, akin to the eternal cosmic cycle.

In conclusion, the influence of mythology on the themes and plotlines of Indian cinema is profound and far-reaching, shaping narratives that resonate with audiences on a deep cultural and spiritual level. Through epic battles, transformative journeys, enduring love stories, moral dilemmas, and spiritual quests, Indian movies draw from the timeless wisdom of ancient myths and legends, enriching contemporary storytelling with the eternal truths of human experience. As Indian cinema continues to evolve and innovate, mythology remains a timeless source of inspiration and a guiding light, illuminating the path of storytelling with its enduring wisdom and universal appeal.

The Use of Mythological Symbols and Motifs:

Mythological symbols and motifs have not only enriched the narratives of ancient scriptures and classical literature but have also found resonance in contemporary Indian literature and cinema. Drawing from the timeless wisdom of mythology, writers and filmmakers continue to infuse their works with these symbols, connecting audiences with the cultural heritage and spiritual legacy of India. Here, we explore some relevant and contemporary examples of the use of mythological symbols and motifs in both literature and cinema:

1. The Lotus:

- **Literature:** In contemporary Indian literature, authors like Arundhati Roy in "The God of Small Things" and Amitav Ghosh in "The Hungry Tide" use the lotus as a symbol of beauty, resilience, and transformation. The lotus serves as a metaphor for the characters' inner struggles and their quest for self-discovery amidst the complexities of life.

- **Cinema:** In the film "Kalank," directed by Abhishek Varman, the lotus pond becomes a recurring motif symbolizing the protagonist's journey of caregiving, selflessness, and personal growth. The serene beauty of the lotus pond reflects the protagonist's inner resilience and her ability to find beauty amidst life's challenges.

2. The Serpent:

- **Literature:** In contemporary Indian literature, authors like Chitra Banerjee Divakaruni in "The Palace of Illusions" and Kiran Nagarkar in "Cuckold" explore the complexities of human relationships and power dynamics through the metaphor of the serpent. The serpent symbolizes desire, temptation, and the darker aspects of human nature.

- **Cinema:** In the film "Nagin," directed by Nandlal Jaswantlal, the serpent motif is used to depict the protagonist's supernatural powers and her quest for vengeance. The film explores themes of love, betrayal, and redemption against the backdrop of ancient folklore and mythology.

3. The Trishul (Trident):

- **Literature:** In contemporary Indian literature, writers like Amish Tripathi in the "Shiva Trilogy" and Devdutt Pattanaik in "My Gita" incorporate the trishul as a symbol of spiritual awakening and inner transformation. The trishul represents the protagonist's journey from ignorance to enlightenment, as they confront their inner demons and embrace their true selves.

- **Cinema:** In the film "Baahubali: The Beginning," directed by S.S. Rajamouli, the trishul is wielded by the protagonist as a symbol of power, courage, and righteousness. The film's epic battle sequences and larger-than-life characters draw inspiration from ancient mythology, captivating audiences with its grandeur and spectacle.

4. The Conch Shell:

- **Literature:** In contemporary Indian literature, authors like Ashwin Sanghi in "The Krishna Key" and Devdutt Pattanaik in "Myth=Mithya" explore the symbolism of the conch shell as a call to action and spiritual awakening.

The conch shell serves as a metaphor for the protagonist's journey of self-discovery and divine revelation.

- **Cinema:** In the film "PK," directed by Rajkumar Hirani, the conch shell is used as a symbol of the protagonist's quest for truth and enlightenment. The film's satirical take on religion and spirituality challenges traditional beliefs and highlights the universal themes of love, compassion, and humanism.

5. The Peacock:

- **Literature:** In contemporary Indian literature, writers like Jhumpa Lahiri in "The Namesake" and Ravi Subramanian in "The Bestseller She Wrote" use the peacock as a symbol of beauty, grace, and aspiration. The peacock symbolizes the protagonist's longing for freedom, creativity, and self-expression.

- **Cinema:** In the film "Padmaavat," directed by Sanjay Leela Bhansali, the peacock motif is used to depict the opulence and grandeur of the Rajputana kingdom. The film's lavish sets and costumes draw inspiration from ancient art and mythology, transporting audiences to a bygone era of romance and valor.

In conclusion, the use of mythological symbols and motifs in contemporary Indian literature and cinema reflects the enduring relevance and cultural resonance of ancient myths and legends. Whether exploring themes of love and redemption or delving into the complexities of human nature and destiny, writers and filmmakers continue to draw inspiration from the rich tapestry of Indian mythology, enriching their narratives with timeless wisdom and universal truths.

xxx~¬~xxx

Key Myths and Stories:

The Creation Myth:

Exploring various creation myths from Indian mythology, including the cosmic egg (Hiranyagarbha) and the emergence of gods and demons from primordial elements. Indian mythology is replete with creation myths that offer explanations for the origins of the universe and the diversity of life forms. These myths often involve cosmic beings, primordial elements, and divine acts of creation, reflecting the ancient Indian worldview and cosmology.

Example: The film "PK" (2014), directed by Rajkumar Hirani, explores themes of creation and spirituality through the lens of satire and comedy. The protagonist, an alien visitor to Earth, questions religious dogma and explores various myths and beliefs in his quest to understand the nature of existence.

The Churning of the Ocean (Samudra Manthan):

The Churning of the Ocean, also known as Samudra Manthan, is a mythological event from Hindu mythology that symbolizes the eternal struggle between gods and demons for supremacy and the quest for immortality. According to the myth, the gods (devas) and demons (asuras) joined forces to churn the cosmic ocean (Samudra) using Mount Mandara as the churning rod and Vasuki, the serpent king, as the rope. The churning resulted in the emergence of various divine treasures, including the elixir of immortality (amrita), which both sides coveted.

During the churning of the ocean, the gods and demons engaged in a titanic struggle, each pulling one end of the serpent Vasuki to churn the ocean. As they churned the waters, Mount Mandara began to sink into the ocean, prompting Lord Vishnu to take the form of Kurma, the turtle avatar, to support the mountain on his back. The churning process unleashed a series of cosmic phenomena and mythical beings. First, a deadly poison known as Halahala emerged from the depths of the ocean, threatening to destroy all creation. To save the world from destruction, Lord Shiva bravely drank the poison, earning him the title of Neelkantha (the blue-throated one).As the churning continued, the ocean yielded various treasures and celestial beings, including Kamadhenu (the wish-fulfilling cow), Ucchaisravas (the divine white horse), and Airavata (the four-tusked elephant). Finally, Dhanvantari, the physician of the gods, emerged carrying the pot of amrita, the elixir of immortality. The myth of the Churning of the Ocean continues to inspire contemporary Indian media forms, including literature, cinema, and television. One notable example is the portrayal of the Samudra Manthan event in the television series "Devon Ke Dev... Mahadev."

In this popular mythological series, which aired from 2011 to 2014, the Churning of the Ocean is depicted with breathtaking visuals and elaborate storytelling. The sequence begins with the gods and demons uniting to churn the ocean in search of the elixir of immortality. As the gods and demons pull on opposite ends of Vasuki, tensions rise, and conflicts ensue.

The series portrays the cosmic significance of the event, highlighting the divine intervention of Lord Vishnu as Kurma and Lord Shiva's sacrifice in drinking the poison to save the world. Through stunning visual effects and powerful performances, the Churning of the Ocean sequence becomes a pivotal moment in the series, showcasing the timeless themes of sacrifice, perseverance, and the triumph of good over evil.

Furthermore, the contemporary retelling of the Churning of the Ocean serves as a reminder of the enduring relevance of ancient myths and legends in shaping the cultural identity and spiritual consciousness of modern India. By weaving together elements of mythology, history, and spirituality, Indian media forms continue to celebrate the rich tapestry of Indian heritage and inspire audiences with timeless tales of courage, sacrifice, and divine intervention.

The Ten Incarnations of Vishnu (DASHAVATAR):

1. **Matsya (The Fish)** - Symbolizes the first life forms in the oceans. In this avatar, Vishnu saves the sacred Vedas

from a deluge that threatens the creation.

2. **Kurma (The Tortoise)** - Represents life forms beginning to inhabit land. Kurma supports the churning of the ocean to obtain amrita (the nectar of immortality), which is a metaphor for showing stability.

3. **Varaha (The Boar)** - Signifies the establishment of terrestrial ecosystems. Varaha rescues the Earth (personified as the goddess Bhudevi) from the demon Hiranyaksha who hides her in the depths of the cosmic ocean.

4. **Narasimha (The Man-Lion)** - Narasimha embodies the transition from animalistic instincts to intellectual and moral pursuits. He

comes forth to destroy the demon Hiranyakashipu, who is beyond the reach of man, beast, or god.

5. **Vamana (The Dwarf)** - Indicates the rise of civilized human beings. Vamana, a Brahmin dwarf, subdues the demon king Bali, a benevolent but ambitious ruler, showing that divine might can conquer physical and material power.

6. **Parashurama (The Warrior with an Axe)** - Reflects the warrior phase of human civilization, where humans begin to establish societal rules and handle complex social dynamics. Parashurama reclaims land from the sea to create Kerala and rids the world of corrupt kshatriyas (warriors) twenty-one times.

7. **Rama (The Prince and King of Ayodhya)** - Represents the ideal human being, embodying virtues like honor, bravery, and morality. Rama's story, detailed in the Ramayana, revolves around his quest to rescue his wife Sita from the demon king Ravana.

8. **Krishna (The Divine Statesman)** - Symbolizes divine diplomacy and ethics in governance. Krishna plays a key role in the Mahabharata, advising the Pandavas and revealing the Bhagavad Gita, a cornerstone of Hindu philosophy, to Arjuna.

9. **Buddha (The Enlightened One)** - Represents intellectual and philosophical refinement. Buddha teaches the path of moderation and compassion, steering away from

extreme asceticism and materialistic bonds.

10. **Kalki (The Mighty Warrior)** - Predicted to appear at the end of the current Kali Yuga (the age of vice), Kalki is believed to come to destroy decadence and restore righteousness, leading to the renewal of the universe.

Chapter 2: Ancient Indian Epics: The Foundation of Mythological Literature

The Ramayana: A Tale of Virtue and Duty:

The Ramayana, one of the two great epics of India, written by sage Valmiki, is not just a story. It is an intricate illustration of morals and duties, reflecting the deep-rooted cultural beliefs of ancient India. At its core, the character of Lord Rama stands as a symbol of virtue and an epitome of manhood, often referred to as 'Maryada Purushottam' which means the perfect man. This exploration delves into how Rama's life and decisions within the Ramayana highlight themes of morality and character development.

1. Upholding Family Honor and Obedience to Parents:

Rama's life is a continual testament to dutifulness, particularly towards one's family. The most striking instance of this is his acceptance of a fourteen-year exile from Ayodhya to uphold his father King Dasharatha's boons to Queen Kaikeyi, his stepmother. Despite the unfairness of the situation, Rama accepts his exile with grace, without any bitterness towards Kaikeyi or his father. This act not only defines the depth of his character but also sets a profound example of filial piety and respect for one's parents' wishes, reflecting the societal norms of that time about duty and respect within the family.

2. Loyalty and Commitment to Spouse:

Rama's relationship with his wife Sita is one of deep love, respect, and commitment. When Sita is abducted by Ravana, Rama goes to great lengths to rescue her, engaging allies like Hanuman and forming an army of vanaras (monkeys) to attack Lanka. This rescue mission is not merely an act of bravery and heroism but is a significant reflection of his unwavering commitment to his wife. His journey to Lanka exemplifies the duty of a husband towards his wife, underscoring the sanctity and importance of marriage in Hindu philosophy.

3. Leadership and Governance:

Another facet of Rama's character is his role as a leader. His interaction with his subjects, his treatment of his allies, and his strategies during the Lanka war demonstrate his capability as a just and effective ruler. A pivotal moment is when he is informed of the public's doubt about Sita's chastity. Despite his personal beliefs, he makes the heart-wrenching decision to abandon her, choosing to place his duty as a king over his desires as a husband. This incident highlights the moral dilemmas faced by a leader and the sacrifices involved in upholding dharma (moral law) and maintaining public trust.

4. Compassion and Forgiveness:

Rama's character is not just about adherence to duty but also about compassion and forgiveness. This is vividly illustrated in his treatment of the vanquished enemy, Ravana. After defeating Ravana, Rama instructs Lakshmana to learn from Ravana, who was a great scholar and an adept ruler despite his moral failings. This act of seeking wisdom from an adversary showcases Rama’s capacity for forgiveness and his recognition of virtue in others, regardless of their faults.

5. *Upholding Truth and Integrity:*

Throughout the epic, Rama faces various challenges that test his resolve to stick to the path of truth and integrity. His entire life can be seen as a series of events that highlight the importance of satya (truth) and dharma in one’s life. For instance, by willingly giving up the throne to uphold his father's promise to Kaikeyi, Rama demonstrates his inherent nature to maintain truth and moral integrity above all personal gains.

6.Personal Sacrifice and the Greater Good:

The theme of personal sacrifice recurs throughout the Ramayana. Rama’s life is full of personal losses and sacrifices made for the greater good of his family and kingdom. From accepting exile to ensure peace in his family to abandoning Sita to uphold the moral standards expected of a king, his life exemplifies the sacrifices required to maintain social and moral order.

In conclusion, Lord Rama's character in the Ramayana is a multidimensional portrayal of an ideal man who embodies the values of truth, duty, righteousness, and compassion. Through his actions and decisions, Rama provides profound insights into the complex interplay of personal desires, moral dilemmas, and societal expectations. The Ramayana thus serves not only as a narrative of adventure and heroism but as a moral compass that guides individuals in understanding and fulfilling their roles within the tapestry of life. Through Rama's life, the epic teaches invaluable lessons about the importance of virtues and duty, which continue to resonate with millions around the world.

The narrative also provides a profound commentary on the principles of Dharma (righteousness) through these characters, offering insights into the human condition and the pursuit of ethical life. Here, we delve deeper into these characters and extract the moral and ethical lessons they impart.

1. Sita - Faithfulness and Sacrifice:

Sita, the consort of Rama, is a figure of immense importance in the Ramayana. Her life and trials speak volumes about faith and purity. Sita's unwavering fidelity to Rama during her abduction by Ravana and her ordeal by fire to prove her chastity highlight her steadfastness and moral fortitude. Sita's trials teach the virtues of faithfulness and the strength of patience and virtue in the face of adversity and suffering.

2. Lakshmana - Devotion and Selflessness:

Lakshmana, Rama's younger brother, is a paradigm of brotherly love and dedication. His decision to accompany Rama into exile voluntarily is a significant sacrifice and shows his unconditional loyalty. Throughout the epic, Lakshmana's actions underscore the ideals of selflessness and loyalty. His protective vigilance over Rama and Sita during their forest stay exemplifies the duty one owes to family and loved ones.

3. Hanuman - Loyalty and Service:

Hanuman, the monkey god, is another central character whose devotion to Rama is legendary. His journey to Lanka, carrying Rama's ring to Sita as a symbol of hope and his subsequent burning of Lanka, demonstrate his bravery, cleverness, and unswerving dedication to Rama. Hanuman teaches the value of true devotion and selfless service in achieving divine goals. His character is a beacon of the power of true devotion and the strength that comes from unwavering faith.

4. Bharata - Righteousness and Dharma:

Bharata, Rama's other brother, is a symbol of dharma and sincerity. Although he was given the throne by his mother Kaikeyi, Bharata's insistence on Rama's return to Ayodhya to take his rightful place as king underscores his deep ethical nature and adherence to duty over personal desire. Bharata's actions teach the importance of righteousness and the need to uphold one's principles even against familial pressures and personal gain.

5. Ravana - Hubris and Redemption:

Ravana, though the antagonist, is a complex character imbued with both valor and vice. A Brahmin and a great scholar, Ravana's abduction of Sita and his subsequent downfall are pivotal to the narrative's moral undertones. Ravana's life warns against the dangers of hubris and unchecked power, illustrating how personal vices can lead to one's demise.

However, his scholarly attributes and his eventual realization of his mistakes also discuss the possibility of redemption and learning, even in one's last moments.

6. Dasharatha - Consequences of Promises:

King Dasharatha, Rama's father, whose promise to Kaikeyi leads to the central crisis of the epic, represents the tragic flaws of a great king. His inability to foresee the consequences of his promises teaches about the importance of prudence and foresight in leadership. Dasharatha's plight is a somber reminder of the weight of promises and the far-reaching ramifications they can have on the lives of others.

Conclusion:

Through these characters, the Ramayana teaches multiple layers of moral complexities and the ethical dilemmas faced by individuals. Each character development arc brings forth lessons on virtue, duty, and the moral struggles inherent in human life. The epic not only entertains but also educates, making it a perennial guide on the path of righteousness. From Rama's example of ideal kingship to Hanuman's devotion and

Bharata's adherence to duty, the Ramayana remains a profound narrative on the conduct of life according to Dharma. Thus, it not only portrays the adventures and challenges of its characters but also serves as a moral compass for generations to come.

The Mahabharata: The Battle of Good and Evil:

The Mahabharata, one of the greatest epics of ancient India, attributed to Sage Vyasa, is a profound narrative of the intricacies of Dharma (righteous duty) juxtaposed against the backdrop of a familial feud that culminates in the epic war of Kurukshetra. It is a story that weaves complex moral issues with the actions of its characters, particularly through the divine figure of Lord Krishna, who steers the course of events and imparts spiritual wisdom. This expansive narrative offers rich insights into the ethical dilemmas and moral struggles faced by these characters.

Lord Krishna: The Divine Charioteer and Guide

Lord Krishna, pivotal to the Mahabharata's theme and narrative, serves as a spiritual guide and charioteer to Arjuna, one of the Pandava brothers. Krishna's role is crucial as he navigates the path of righteousness and imparts the sacred text of the Bhagavad Gita, encapsulating the philosophical core of the epic.

1. Krishna's Counsel in the Bhagavad Gita:

On the battlefield of Kurukshetra, as Arjuna faces his own relatives, teachers, and friends on the opposing side, he is beset with doubt and moral confusion about fighting in the war. Krishna imparts to Arjuna the essential spiritual guidance through the Bhagavad Gita, teaching him about various paths to righteousness and the nature of duty. Krishna explains the importance of performing one's duty without attachment to results, which is a fundamental tenet of Karmic philosophy.

2. *Strategy and Non-Attachment:*

Krishna's strategies throughout the war underscore a complex understanding of morality and ethics. He advocates for acting according to one's Dharma, even when it involves trickery and deceit, as long as it serves the greater good. This is evident in his advice to Yudhishthira to lie to Drona about the death of his son, which eventually leads to Drona's downfall. This act, controversial in its nature, challenges conventional morality and compels the reader to reflect on the balance between righteousness and necessity.

The Pandavas and Their Trials

The Pandava brothers, each embodying distinct virtues, face numerous challenges that test their character and moral fiber.

1. Yudhishthira: Adherence to Dharma:

Yudhishthira, the eldest Pandava, is a paragon of virtue and adheres strictly to

Dharma. His moral dilemma during the game of dice, where he gambles away his kingdom, his brothers, and even his wife Draupadi, serves as a critical study of the conflict between adherence to one's word and moral righteousness. His subsequent journey to redemption is a pivotal theme of the epic.

2. Bhima: Strength and Loyalty:

Bhima's immense physical strength is matched by his fierce loyalty to his family. His character development is seen as he avenges the humiliation of Draupadi by slaying Dushasana, reflecting the themes of justice and retribution.

3. Arjuna: The Reluctant Warrior:

Arjuna's journey is one of spiritual growth and self-realization. His initial reluctance to fight in the battle is transformed into a resolved warrior guided by Krishna's teachings. Arjuna's struggles highlight the inner conflict faced by individuals when duty calls for them to act against their own kin.

Kauravas and the Flaw of Ambition

The Kauravas, especially Duryodhana, embody the flaws of unchecked ambition and envy. Duryodhana's refusal to share the kingdom peacefully with the Pandavas, driven by jealousy and pride, sets the stage for the epic conflict.

1. Duryodhana: Power and Pride:

Duryodhana's character is a study in the corrupting power of ambition and the destructive nature of envy. His actions, motivated by a desire to usurp the Pandavas' rightful claim to the throne, illustrate the dangers of moral corruption.

2. Shakuni: Manipulation and Deceit:

Shakuni, uncle to the Kauravas, plays a crucial role as the mastermind behind many of the schemes against the Pandavas. His cunning and deceit serve as a foil to the moral virtues upheld by the Pandavas and Krishna, highlighting the darker aspects of human nature.

Draupadi: The Feminine Force of Justice:

Draupadi, the wife of the Pandavas, is a complex character who often drives the narrative forward. Her humiliation in the Kaurava court where none came to her rescue except Krishna, who miraculously ensured that her honor remained intact, sparks a major turning point in the epic. Draupadi's quest for justice and her unwavering determination highlight the strength of righteous indignation and the resilience to seek retribution in the face of adversity.

Contemporary Teachings Through the Character of Lord Krishna:

Lord Krishna's role transcends the ancient battlefield of Kurukshetra, reaching into the heart of modern ethical dilemmas and providing a guide for right action in today's complex world. His teachings in the Bhagavad Gita and his actions throughout the Mahabharata resonate with timeless relevance.

1. The Concept of Righteous Action Without Attachment:

One of the central teachings of Krishna is the concept of 'Nishkama Karma', or action without desire for its fruits. This principle is especially pertinent in today's fast-paced, result-oriented world. Krishna's counsel to perform one's duty without emotional attachment to the outcomes encourages a focus on duty rather than personal gain. This can be applied in contemporary settings like workplaces or in leadership, where ethical decision-making requires putting collective needs above personal rewards.

2. Dharma (Righteous Duty) Versus Personal Desires:

Krishna's discussions about Dharma in the Gita provide a framework for understanding one's role and responsibilities in life. He argues that one's duty (sva-dharma) is sacred and should not be neglected, even when personal conflicts arise. This teaching helps individuals navigate their responsibilities in family, career, and society, encouraging them to act according to their roles and capabilities, rather than subjective desires. This can aid in resolving conflicts where personal interests clash with professional or social duties.

3. Justice and Forgiveness:

Krishna's interactions with various characters show a deep commitment to justice, tempered with compassion and forgiveness. For example, his strategy in dealing with the aggressive tactics of the Kauravas and his final advice to forgive them highlight the importance of justice in maintaining social order and the power of forgiveness to heal and rebuild communities. This dual approach can guide contemporary issues like criminal justice reforms, where balancing justice and rehabilitation is crucial.

4. Leadership and Governance:

Krishna as a statesman and advisor illustrates ideal leadership qualities: wisdom, integrity, and the ability to make tough decisions for the greater good. His role as a guide to Arjuna, imparting knowledge and facilitating tough but righteous decisions, serves as a model for leaders in all spheres today. His teachings emphasize the importance of vision, ethical governance, and the welfare of all stakeholders, ideals pertinent to modern political and corporate leadership.

5. The Unity of Various Paths to the Divine:

Krishna expounds on various yogic paths to realization — Karma Yoga (path of action), Bhakti Yoga (path of devotion), and Jnana Yoga (path of knowledge). This pluralism in spiritual paths offers a broad view that can accommodate diverse religious and spiritual practices in our globalized world, promoting tolerance and understanding across different faiths and beliefs.

6. Embracing Change and the Impermanence of Life:

Krishna teaches about the transient nature of life and the universe through the concept of Maya (illusion) and the impermanence of material existence. This worldview can help contemporary societies cope with the constant change and uncertainties of modern life, encouraging flexibility, resilience, and a focus on spiritual over material wealth.

Conclusion:

Lord Krishna's character in the Mahabharata is a repository of wisdom and guidance on leading a life aligned with universal virtues of truth, duty, and justice. His teachings in the Bhagavad Gita are particularly relevant in addressing the moral and ethical dilemmas of the modern world — from the struggles of individual duty and ethics to broader social justice issues.

Through the narratives and dialogues of Krishna and the other characters, the Mahabharata remains a profound influence on not only Indian culture but also on the philosophical underpinnings of contemporary thought worldwide. It offers enduring lessons on how to live rightly in a world rife with conflict, challenges, and complexities. The epic encourages a reflective approach to life's trials and tribulations, promoting a balanced and righteous path forward for individuals seeking to navigate the moral landscapes of their lives.

xxx~¬~xxx

The Puranas: Cosmic Tales of Creation and Destruction:

The Puranas are ancient Hindu texts that play a pivotal role in the cultural and spiritual landscape of India. They are an extensive collection of stories, hymns, and philosophies that discuss the universe's creation, preservation, and ultimate destruction. These texts serve as a foundational cornerstone for Indian mythology, offering profound insights into the cosmic and moral order. Here, we explore the depths of the Puranas, their narratives on creation and destruction, and their enduring teachings relevant to contemporary society.

Understanding the Puranas:

The Puranas are a genre of important Hindu religious texts that include myths, legends, and traditional lore, which can be divided into several types such as the Mahapuranas and Upapuranas. Among the most famous are the Bhagavata Purana, which focuses on the avatars of

Vishnu, particularly Krishna; the Shiva Purana, dedicated to the legends and rituals associated with Lord Shiva; and the Devi Bhagavata Purana, which extols the goddess Devi.

These texts use stories of divine figures to convey moral and philosophical truths, exploring themes such as creation, cosmology, genealogy, and the epochs of the world as understood within Hindu tradition.

The Cosmic Cycle of Creation and Destruction:

The Puranas present a cyclical view of the universe which is eternally recreated and destroyed. This cyclical process, known as samsara, is divided into four ages (Yugas): Satya Yuga, Treta Yuga, Dvapara Yuga, and Kali Yuga. These cycles describe the gradual decline of human virtue and morality, starting from a golden age of purity to a dark age of corruption.

1. Satya Yuga (Age of Truth): The first Yuga is the age of truth and perfection, which lasted for 1,728,000 years. The Puranas depict this era as a time of honesty, virtue, and ideal living conditions where malice and deceit are nonexistent.

2. Treta Yuga: The second age sees a minor decline from the ideal state of the previous age, with virtue still predominant but with the emergence of human imperfections. It lasts 1,296,000 years.

3. Dvapara Yuga: Marked by further decline in righteousness and human values, this third age lasts 864,000 years. The events of the Mahabharata, including the life and teachings of Krishna, are said to occur during this era.

4. Kali Yuga (Age of Kali): The final age is characterized by strife, ignorance, irreligion, and vice. It is supposed to last 432,000 years and is the current age according to Hindu cosmology. This period's darkness is broken by the eventual appearance of Kalki, a savior avatar who will usher in a new Satya Yuga, thus restarting the cycle.

Philosophical and Moral Lessons:

The narratives found in the Puranas are rich with philosophical insights and moral lessons that are highly relevant even in modern contexts.

1. The Nature of Dharma: The Puranas extensively discuss Dharma (righteousness), portraying it as a multifaceted concept that evolves over the yugas. The texts emphasize the importance of adhering to one's dharma according to their stage of life, societal role, and cosmic era. This adaptability of dharma offers a framework for ethical decision-making in contemporary, diverse societies.

2. **Karma and Reincarnation:** A central doctrine in the Puranas is karma, the law of cause and effect. Actions in one's life are believed to determine their fate in future reincarnations. This notion supports the idea of moral responsibility and ethical conduct in the present.

3. **Unity in Diversity:** The Puranas illustrate a cosmos teeming with diverse deities, creatures, and worlds, promoting a view that unity and harmony can exist amid diversity. This teaching is particularly poignant in today's globalized

world, emphasizing tolerance and coexistence among different cultures and religions.

4. Environmental Consciousness: Many stories in the Puranas highlight the interdependence between humans and nature, suggesting a form of environmental ethics. This resonates with contemporary issues of ecological conservation and sustainable living.

5. The Role of Rituals and Festivals: The Puranas also codify numerous Hindu rituals and festivals that bind communities together. These rituals are not only religious practices but also opportunities for social cohesion and cultural education, relevant to preserving identity in an increasingly homogenized world.

Conclusion:

The Puranas not only narrate cosmic cycles of creation and destruction but also embed deep ethical and philosophical teachings within these tales. Their narratives help illuminate the complex dynamics of human behavior, societal structures, and universal truths. By fostering an understanding of dharma, karma and cosmic justice, they offer valuable insights for personal growth and communal harmony.

The Significance of Devotion :

One of the pivotal teachings in many Puranas, especially prominent in the Bhagavata Purana, is the path of Bhakti (devotion). This path emphasizes devotion towards a personal god as a means to achieve spiritual liberation and happiness. The stories of devotees such as Prahlada, who remained devoted to Vishnu despite severe trials, or the gopis of Vrindavan, whose unconditional love for Krishna transcends the mundane, inspire followers to cultivate sincerity and faith in divine grace.

Contemporary Relevance:

In today's fast-paced world, where existential anxieties and materialistic concerns often lead to spiritual disorientation, the Bhakti movement's teachings offer a way to find inner peace and purpose through devotion and surrender. This approach can help alleviate modern stresses and provide a deep sense of fulfillment and stability in one's life.

Moral Agency and Leadership:

The Puranas also explore the themes of leadership and governance through narratives about kings and divine heroes who embody ideal qualities. For instance, King Rama in the Ramayana (often included in the Puranic corpus) is revered not just for his bravery but for his selfless dedication to Dharma. Similarly, Yudhishthira from the Mahabharata is depicted as a model of ethical governance.

Contemporary Relevance:

These characters provide enduring lessons on the importance of ethical leadership and the virtues required to sustain it, such as integrity, justice, and compassion. In a world plagued by political corruption and leadership crises, the Puranic ideals can serve as ethical benchmarks for leaders in all spheres of life.

Understanding Suffering and Liberation:

The concept of suffering and the pursuit of liberation (Moksha) are extensively discussed in the Puranas. They teach that life's trials and tribulations are due to past karmas and that true liberation comes from spiritual knowledge and detachment. The story of King Bharata, who becomes attached to a deer and forgets his spiritual practices, highlights the dangers of worldly attachments.

Contemporary Relevance:

These teachings are vital in addressing the modern dilemma of attachment to material success and sensory pleasures. The Puranic philosophy encourages a balanced life where spiritual well-being is given priority, promoting mental health and holistic living.

Cultural and Social Wisdom:

The Puranas are treasure troves of cultural and social wisdom, detailing various rites of passage, community festivals, and social norms. These elements play a crucial role in maintaining the social fabric of Hindu communities worldwide.

Contemporary Relevance:

In multicultural societies, understanding and participating in the cultural practices of different communities can promote inclusiveness and respect for diversity. The rituals and festivals detailed in the Puranas provide opportunities for non-Hindus to learn about and engage with Hindu traditions, fostering intercultural dialogue and mutual respect.

Environmental and Cosmic Harmony:

Several Puranas, like the Matsya Purana and the Bhagavata Purana, narrate tales where the environment and the cosmos are integral to the divine plan. The respect for all forms of life and the emphasis on the balance of nature encapsulated in these stories are increasingly relevant in light of global ecological crises.

Contemporary Relevance:

These narratives can inspire modern environmental movements, emphasizing sustainability and respect for biodiversity as key components of spiritual and worldly life. They provide a profound understanding that human well-being is deeply connected to the health of the planet.

Conclusion:

The Puranas, with their rich narratives of creation, preservation, and destruction, are not only foundational texts for understanding Hindu mythology but also sources of timeless wisdom. Their teachings on Dharma, devotion, leadership, and the importance of ecological and social harmony continue to resonate deeply in today's world. By studying these texts, contemporary societies can glean lessons on living a balanced, ethical, and spiritually fulfilled life. In this way, the ancient Puranas continue to serve as a guiding light for personal conduct and societal ethics, showing how age-old wisdom can address even the most modern challenges.

Chapter 3: The Impact of Indian Mythology in Contemporary Literature

Novels, Short Stories and Contemporary Literature Inspired by Mythology, Mythological Retellings and Adaptations:

Indian mythology, with its rich tapestry of gods, goddesses, heroes, and demons, has inspired countless writers to reinterpret these ancient tales for modern audiences. From the philosophical depths of the Bhagavad Gita to the epic narratives of the Ramayana and Mahabharata, these stories have been reimagined in various forms, influencing literature, cinema, and popular culture globally. This exploration delves into how contemporary novels and short stories have been inspired by Indian mythology and the significant impact they have had on readers and cultures around the world.

Redefining Epic Narratives:

Contemporary authors have taken the complex narratives and characters from Indian epics and recontextualized them into modern settings, exploring timeless themes of duty, courage, morality, and spirituality. These reinterpretations often focus on lesser-known characters or retell the stories from alternative perspectives, providing fresh insights into well-known events.

1. The Palace of Illusions by Chitra Banerjee Divakaruni:

This novel retells the Mahabharata from the perspective of Draupadi, the complex and formidable heroine of the epic. By narrating the story through Draupadi's eyes, Divakaruni offers a feminist angle to the traditional tale, highlighting the struggles and injustices faced by women in a patriarchal society. This retelling has resonated with readers worldwide, sparking discussions about gender roles and equality.

2. Asura: Tale of the Vanquished by Anand Neelakantan:

Neelakantan's book tells the story of the Ramayana from the point of view of Ravana, the epic's antagonist. This novel challenges the traditional dichotomy of good vs. evil, suggesting that history is often written by the victors. "Asura" explores themes of class injustice and the complexity of human nature, which are highly relevant in today's society.

Exploring New Genres and Formats:

Modern writers have not only revisited the narratives but have also experimented with various literary genres and formats to make these ancient myths accessible and relevant to contemporary readers. This includes fantasy, science fiction, and even graphic novels.

1. Shiva Trilogy by Amish Tripathi:

Amish Tripathi's books blend mythological narrative with fantasy elements, creating an enthralling fictional world where gods behave like human beings and face earthly challenges. This series has been particularly popular among young readers, introducing them to mythical stories in a format that is exciting and relatable.

2. Krishna Udayasankar's Aryavarta Chronicles:

Udayasankar's trilogy is a retelling of the Mahabharata set in a realistic historical framework, stripping away the divine elements to focus on political intrigue and human drama. This approach has appealed to fans of historical and political thrillers, showing how versatile these ancient tales can be.

Retelling in Indian Cinema:

- **"Tumbbad" (2018)** is a notable example of Indian cinema that intricately weaves mythology with horror and fantasy to explore themes of greed, human nature, and the eternal quest for immortality. Directed by Rahi Anil Barve and Adesh Prasad, "Tumbbad" is set in the 20th century in the village of Tumbbad, Maharashtra, and spans several decades, presenting a gripping narrative steeped in folklore and supernatural elements. Tumbbad stands as a testament to how Indian cinema can effectively use folklore and mythology not only to tell engaging stories but also to reflect on the human condition through powerful metaphors and narratives.

- **"RRR" (2022)** is an Indian film directed by S.S. Rajamouli, a cinematic spectacle that, while not a direct adaptation of any specific mythological tale, creatively incorporates elements of Indian mythology to enhance its narrative and thematic depth.

The film draws a symbolic parallel between the characters and the figures of Lord Rama and Hanuman from the Ramayana. Alluri Sitarama Raju, characterized as a stoic leader and a skilled archer, mirrors Lord Rama. In contrast, Komaram Bheem, with his raw strength, loyalty, and protective nature, reflects Hanuman's attributes. Their bond in the film symbolizes the deep, brotherly love and respect shared between Rama and Hanuman, emphasizing themes of loyalty, bravery, and sacrifice.

"RRR" reimagines elements of Indian mythology within a historical framework, using the powerful imagery and themes of ancient epics to craft a compelling narrative about freedom and friendship.

- **"Kantara" (2022)** The 2022 Indian film "Kantara," written and directed by Rishab Shetty, who also stars as the lead, is a powerful narrative steeped in folklore and regional mythology. Set in a small village in Karnataka, the film weaves a compelling tale that revolves around the conflict between man and nature, a theme deeply rooted in Indian mythological traditions.
  "Kantara" translates the sacred tradition of 'Bhoota Kola,' a ritualistic folk dance performed in parts of Karnataka, into its narrative core. The protagonist, Shiva, plays a significant role in this ritual, which is believed to be a divine dance where humans commune with the spirits. This ritual

is a medium for divine justice, bridging the human and spiritual worlds, reminiscent of many mythological narratives where deities intervene in mortal affairs. The film portrays the forest as a living entity, almost a deity that demands respect and reverence, which echoes the Indian mythological reverence for nature.

The spirit guardian of the village, who becomes a central figure in resolving the conflict over land and justice, is reminiscent of the guardian deities often found in Hindu mythology, who protect their devotees and maintain cosmic balance.

"Kantara" creatively retells elements of Indian mythology through its exploration of folk traditions, spiritual beliefs, and the profound connection between humans and nature. It highlights the consequences of disrupting the sacred balance, emphasizing themes of duty, respect, and the cyclical nature of life and justice.

- **"Dasavathaaram,"** a 2008 Indian film directed by K.S. Ravikumar and starring Kamal Haasan, is a unique cinematic endeavor that intertwines the ten avatars of Lord Vishnu with contemporary narratives across various timelines. This film does not directly retell the traditional stories of Vishnu's avatars but ingeniously uses the concept to parallel ten different characters, all portrayed by Kamal Haasan, whose stories converge in a modern setting, reflecting the philosophical and cultural dimensions of the avatars.

  Each of the ten characters played by Kamal Haasan symbolizes one of

Vishnu's avatars, adapting their core characteristics to modern scenarios. For example, the character Balram Naidu, a RAW operative, mimics the strength and strategic acumen of Balarama; the scientist Govindarajan represents the Matsya avatar, trying to prevent a bioweapon calamity much like Matsya saved the Vedas from being destroyed.

"Dasavathaaram" artfully uses the mythological template of the Dashavatara to weave a complex narrative that spans various eras and geographies, bringing ancient wisdom to bear on modern dilemmas. Through its innovative storytelling, the film explores the eternal battle between good and evil, chaos and order, and the enduring need for preservation and renewal. Each character, embodying traits of the avatars, highlights the timeless relevance of these mythological themes, making "Dasavathaaram" a thought-provoking reflection on the cyclical nature of human challenges and divine intervention.

Impact on Cultural Discourse:

These contemporary retellings of Indian mythology have played a significant role in shaping cultural discourse, both in India and internationally. They have prompted readers to reconsider moral and philosophical questions, understand different cultural contexts, and explore complex human emotions.

1. Feminism and Gender Studies:

Books like "The Palace of Illusions" have inspired discussions on feminism, showcasing how ancient myths can be relevant in highlighting current gender issues. By focusing on female characters who were often sidelined in traditional narratives, these stories promote a greater understanding of women's roles in both historical and modern contexts.

2. Philosophy and Ethics:

Many modern retellings incorporate philosophical reflections, mirroring the introspective nature of texts like the Bhagavad Gita. For example, "Asura" and the "Shiva Trilogy" encourage readers to explore ethical dilemmas and personal philosophies, prompting a reflection on one's moral compass.

Promoting Cross-Cultural Understanding:

The global popularity of these novels has helped in promoting cross-cultural understanding. By presenting Indian myths in formats that are universally relatable—such as fantasy, drama, or moral dilemmas—they attract a diverse audience who might not otherwise engage with Indian culture.

1. International Reach and Adaptations:

These mythological stories have been translated into multiple languages, reaching a global audience. They have also been adapted into films, television series, and even stage plays, further expanding their influence and fostering an appreciation for Indian cultural heritage worldwide.

2. Educational Impact:

In educational contexts, these stories are used to introduce students to Indian culture and philosophical ideas. They serve as a bridge between contemporary life and ancient wisdom, helping students understand global cultures and histories.

Influence on Other Media:

The impact of these novelistic retellings extends beyond literature into films, television, and digital media, where they influence how stories are told and understood.

1. Cinema and Television:

Indian cinema, including Bollywood and regional film industries, has frequently adapted mythological tales. These adaptations have often drawn from the narrative styles and character interpretations seen in contemporary novels. Films and TV series like Hanu-man, Adipurush, RRR, Ramayana, Mahabharata are influenced by such novels, using similar themes of moral complexity and heroic struggles. These adaptations have not only been successful domestically but have also garnered international fame, showcasing Indian storytelling on a global stage.

2. Web Series and Online Platforms:

The advent of digital streaming platforms has further broadened the scope for retelling these ancient myths. Series such as "Sacred Games" and "Asur" incorporate mythological motifs and lessons into modern-day narratives, blending crime, drama, and philosophy. These shows have captivated a global audience, demonstrating the universal appeal and flexibility of Indian mythological themes.

3. Video Games and Virtual Reality:

Emerging technologies such as video games and virtual reality offer new mediums for experiencing these age-old stories. Games that use Indian mythological settings and characters allow players to engage interactively with these narratives, providing a deeper understanding and appreciation of their themes.

Contemporary Social and Political Commentary:

Many modern authors use mythological retellings to comment on current social and political issues, making ancient myths relevant to today's societal challenges.

1. Social Justice and Inequality:

Books like Asura and The Palace of Illusions highlight issues of social justice, caste inequality, and power dynamics, drawing parallels between the societal structures of mythical times and contemporary issues. These narratives encourage readers to reflect on and question the prevailing social norms and injustices in their own worlds.

2. Nationalism and Cultural Identity:

In countries like India, where mythology is deeply intertwined with national identity, these stories often foster a sense of pride and cultural continuity. They are sometimes used in political discourse to underscore certain ideologies or values, influencing public opinion and national policy discussions.

Literary and Artistic Innovations:

The infusion of Indian mythology into modern literature has also spurred innovations in narrative and artistic expression, influencing writers and artists around the world.

1. Narrative Techniques:

Writers like Neil Gaiman, who penned The Sandman series, have acknowledged the influence of world mythologies, including Indian, on their storytelling techniques. These authors blend myth with contemporary issues, using complex narrative structures and character arcs inspired by the epics.

2. Art and Design:

Illustrators and graphic designers often draw upon the rich visual imagery of Indian mythology when creating artwork for books, comics, films, and video games. The vibrant depictions of deities, monsters, and epic battles in these media are directly inspired by the descriptions found in the Puranas and other mythological texts.

Educational and Psychological Impact:

The reinterpretation of Indian myths has also had significant educational and psychological effects, helping individuals navigate personal and existential questions.

1. Moral and Ethical Education:

These stories are often used in moral and ethical education, helping individuals develop a sense of right and wrong through the complex characters and plots of mythological narratives. They provide a rich resource for discussing ethical dilemmas and personal values in schools and communities.

2. Psychological Resilience:

Engaging with complex mythological narratives can help build psychological resilience. Characters who overcome adversity and moral trials provide models for coping with personal challenges, encouraging readers to develop resilience in the face of their own difficulties.

Conclusion:

Novels and short stories inspired by Indian mythology have profoundly impacted contemporary literature and popular culture, offering new ways to engage with ancient stories that are imbued with deep moral and philosophical meanings. These modern adaptations have not only rejuvenated interest in Indian mythology but have also facilitated a global dialogue about cultural heritage, ethical dilemmas, and personal identity.

By reframing traditional narratives to reflect contemporary issues and ideas, these works encourage a reevaluation of moral values and societal norms. They challenge readers worldwide to consider complex questions about justice, duty, and righteousness in a modern context. As these stories continue to inspire new interpretations and adaptations, their influence extends through generations, shaping how we understand not only the past but also the present and future of our global society.

xxx~¬~xxx

The Tales of Panchatantra: Lessons in Morality and their Impact:

The Panchatantra, an ancient Indian collection of interrelated animal fables in verse and prose, is one of the most widely translated non-religious books in history. The original text, written in Sanskrit by Vishnu Sharma around 300 BCE, was intended to instruct the sons of a king in the ways of the world and is a quintessential example of the niti (moral wisdom) literature. Each story is accompanied by a moral that has not only made a significant impact on Indian mythology but has also offered valuable lessons that are relevant in today's global society.

Origins and Structure:

The Panchatantra is structured into five books, each containing a series of stories that are interconnected by characters and themes. These five books are:

- **Mitra-bheda:** The Book of Uniting Friends
- **Mitra-lābha or Mitra-samprāpti:** The Book of Gaining Friends

- **Kākolūkīyam:** The Book of Crows and Owls
- **Labdhapraṇāśam:** The Book of Loss of Gains
- **Aparīkṣitakārakaṁ:** The Book of Rash Actions

These tales use the format of a frame story, where one story is narrated within another, to teach ethical and moral lessons centered around political science and personal conduct.

Impact on Indian Mythology:

The Panchatantra's stories have been influential in shaping the narrative structure and moral ethos of later Indian literature, including the Puranas and the epic narratives of the Mahabharata and Ramayana. These tales emphasize the practical aspects of life and teach how intelligence, presence of mind, and wisdom can triumph over brute force and naivety.

1. Moral and Ethical Teachings:

The narratives focus heavily on practical advice rather than on abstract philosophical concepts. This has helped embed a pragmatic sense of morality into Indian culture, influencing its rich storytelling tradition.

2. Influence on Other Literary Works:

The structure and storytelling techniques found in the Panchatantra have inspired numerous other works within Indian literature and folklore. The use of animals to convey human virtues and vices has been particularly impactful, providing a safe vessel to explore complex human behaviors.

Contemporary Learnings and Global Influence:

The universal lessons contained in the Panchatantra have transcended cultural and geographical boundaries, making them relevant even in contemporary times.

1. Lessons in Governance and Leadership:

Many stories in the Panchatantra revolve around themes of governance and leadership. For example, the story of the lion and the rabbit that teaches about the dangers of hasty decisions is often used to illustrate the importance of wise and measured leadership in political and corporate scenarios.

2. Conflict Resolution and Negotiation:

The Panchatantra teaches how to navigate conflict and negotiate successfully, skills that are invaluable in the modern world. The tales often demonstrate the benefits of diplomacy and dialogue over warfare and conflict, which can be applied in both personal and professional lives.

3. Psychological Insight and Human Behavior:

The stories offer insights into human psychology and the complexities of human behavior. By analyzing the actions of the characters, readers learn about the motives driving behavior and how to deal with different personalities, which is useful for psychological understanding and social interactions.

Modern Adaptations and Media:

Over the years, the Panchatantra has been adapted into various formats across different media, significantly impacting children's literature and moral education worldwide.

1. Children's Books and Educational Tools:

The straightforward moral lessons of the Panchatantra have made it a popular choice for children's books and educational cartoons. These adaptations are used globally in schools and homes to teach values such as honesty, integrity, and resourcefulness.

2. Animation and Film:

Numerous animated films and television shows have been inspired by the Panchatantra, helping to instill ethical values and life skills in young viewers. These media adaptations have extended the reach of the Panchatantra's lessons, making them accessible to a global audience.

3. Video Games and Interactive Media:

Interactive media like video games have also begun exploring narratives based on the Panchatantra, allowing players to engage with the stories and their morals in an interactive environment. This format helps in teaching strategic thinking and moral decision-making.

Influence on World Literature:

The Panchatantra has had a significant influence not only on Indian literature but also on world literature. The fables have been translated into numerous languages and have influenced folk tale traditions around the world.

1. Middle Eastern and Western Adaptations:

The Panchatantra was translated into Persian by Borzuya in 570 CE as Kalīla wa Dimna and later into Arabic in the same name by Abdullah Ibn al-Muqaffa during the 8th century. These versions then served as the basis for translations into Hebrew, Latin, and eventually into most European languages. The tales have influenced a wide array of Western literary works, including the fables of

Aesop, the Gesta Romanorum, and even the works of La Fontaine.

2. Influence on Other Cultural Folktales:

The structure and morals of the Panchatantra have parallels in folklore across Asia and Europe. For instance, many of the moral lessons and story mechanisms can be seen in the Canterbury Tales by Geoffrey Chaucer and the fables of Bidpai. Through these widespread adaptations, the Panchatantra's impact can be seen in moral and ethical teachings across multiple cultures, highlighting its universal relevance and appeal.

Ethical and Moral Considerations in Contemporary Society:

The timeless wisdom encapsulated in the Panchatantra continues to offer ethical guidelines and moral reflections that are pertinent to contemporary societal issues.

1. Ethical Leadership and Integrity:

In a world rife with corruption and leadership crises, the Panchatantra's emphasis on wise and ethical leadership is particularly relevant. Stories such as those involving the judicious elephant king or the wise crow leader serve as allegorical reminders of the qualities necessary for good leadership, including fairness, intelligence, and the moral courage to do what is right.

2. The Importance of Cleverness and Wisdom:

In today's complex global environment, the qualities of cleverness and strategic thinking are as important as ever. The Panchatantra's tales often highlight the triumph of brains over brawn and the importance of wit in overcoming adversity. These stories encourage creative problem-solving and underscore the value of intelligence and adaptability in both personal and professional realms.

3. Social Harmony and Conflict Resolution:

Many stories in the Panchatantra revolve around themes of conflict resolution and the maintenance of social harmony. Through tales involving negotiations between animals of different species, the stories promote values of tolerance, understanding, and peace-making. These narratives can serve as useful metaphors for addressing and resolving modern social and interpersonal conflicts.

Psychological and Educational Impact:

The psychological depth and educational value of the Panchatantra's stories make them an enduring tool for teaching and learning about human nature and social dynamics.

1. Understanding Human Motivations:

The Panchatantra provides deep insights into human motivations and behaviors, portrayed through the actions of anthropomorphized animal characters. These stories can be used in educational settings to help children and adults alike understand complex psychological concepts in a simplified and relatable manner.

2. Moral Development in Children:

By presenting moral dilemmas and ethical questions, the Panchatantra plays a crucial role in the moral development of young readers. These stories help children learn about virtue, justice, and ethical reasoning, which are essential for personal growth and development.

3. Use in Therapeutic and Counseling Environments:

The universal themes and accessible narratives of the Panchatantra also make it a valuable resource in therapeutic and counseling settings. Psychologists and counselors often use these stories as tools to help clients explore personal issues, resolve psychological conflicts, and achieve greater self-awareness.

Cultural Preservation and Global Exchange:

The global dissemination and enduring popularity of the Panchatantra highlight its role in cultural preservation and exchange. Through its various translations and adaptations, the Panchatantra has become a vehicle for promoting cultural dialogue and understanding across borders.

1. Promoting Indian Cultural Values:

As one of India's greatest literary contributions to the world, the

Panchatantra plays a significant role in promoting Indian cultural values and philosophical insights globally. Its stories are imbued with the teachings of Hindu philosophy and the practical wisdom of ancient Indian civilization, offering a window into the country's rich cultural heritage.

2. Fostering Intercultural Learning:

The widespread popularity of the Panchatantra across different cultures and languages facilitates intercultural learning and understanding. By engaging with these stories, readers from various cultural backgrounds are introduced to universal moral questions and human values, promoting a sense of shared humanity and mutual respect.

Conclusion:

The Tales of the Panchatantra are not only a collection of entertaining stories but also a profound source of moral and philosophical wisdom. Their impact on Indian mythology is significant, but their influence extends far beyond—into the realms of global literature, ethical philosophy,psychological understanding, and educational methodologies. In an increasingly complex and interconnected world, the timeless lessons of the Panchatantra continue to provide valuable insights into human nature, societal dynamics, and the universal quest for wisdom and virtue.

xxx~¬~xxx

Mythological Folk Songs and Poetry, The Use of Gods and Goddesses as Literary Symbols:

Indian mythology, rich with gods, goddesses, and legendary heroes, provides a fertile ground for cultural expressions through folk songs and poetry. These art forms have not only served to preserve traditional narratives but also to interpret divine attributes into symbols of human values and aspirations. This essay explores how these mythological figures are utilized as literary symbols in Indian folk culture and their continuing relevance in contemporary society.

Symbolism in Mythological Folk Songs and Poetry:

1. Gods and Goddesses as Archetypes:

In Indian folk songs and poetry, deities are often portrayed not just as divine figures but also as archetypes symbolizing various human qualities and existential concepts.

For example: Lord Krishna is frequently symbolized as a figure of love and divine joy. His playful antics with the Gopis (milkmaids), as depicted in many folk songs, represent an allegory of the soul's joyous union with the divine. Goddess Durga is portrayed as a symbol of strength and empowerment, her battles representing the fight against ignorance and evil.

2. Literary Symbolism in Folk Narratives:

Folk songs and poems use these deities to address social issues, philosophical questions, and personal emotions. For instance, Shiva's dance of destruction and creation in classical Indian poetry symbolizes the cyclic nature of life and the universe, reflecting beliefs about death and rebirth that resonate with philosophical existentialism.

Examples from Diverse Cultural Backgrounds:

1. Hindu Influence:

- *Tulsidas*, famous for his epic poem Ramcharitmanas, used Lord Rama as a central figure symbolizing righteousness and moral integrity. His works are pivotal in promoting devotion (Bhakti) in Hindi literature.

- *Vidyapati*, known for his lyrical poetry in Maithili, extensively used imagery of Shiva and Parvati to express the human yearning for the divine.

- *Meera Bai,* a 16th-century Rajput princess and poet, is known for her deep devotion to Lord Krishna, depicted through her poems. In her verses, Krishna is not just a mythological deity but also a symbol of the ultimate lover, representing divine love that transcends the physical and material. Her poetry uses Krishna as a metaphor for the soul's intense longing and devotion to the divine, showcasing her spiritual journey through Bhakti (devotion).

- *Ramdhari Singh Dinkar*, a modern Hindi poet, used characters like Karna from the Mahabharata to comment on the human condition and dilemmas faced by individuals in society. His epic poem Rashmirathi focuses on Karna's life and the moral challenges he faces, reflecting on themes of fate, duty, and righteousness that resonate with contemporary issues of identity and moral integrity.

2. Muslim Influence:

- *Abdul Rahim Khan-I-Khana*, also known as Rahim, used moral vignettes involving human characters and sometimes deities like Krishna to illustrate practical aspects of life and ethics in his couplets.

- *Sant Kabir*, a 15th-century mystic poet and saint, often used Lord Rama in his dohas (couplets) to symbolize God as the ultimate truth and reality. Kabir's poetry, while drawing on Hindu concepts, speaks to a universal audience, emphasizing Rama not just as a Hindu deity but as a spiritual anchor in a world of moral and social upheaval.

3. Sikh Influence:

Guru Nanak, the founder of Sikhism, wrote hymns that often referenced Hindu mythology to convey messages of equality and devotion. His poetry is included in the Guru Granth Sahib, the holy scripture of Sikhism.

4. Regional Poets Across Languages:

- *Namdev* and *Tukaram* in Marathi, Surdas in Braj, and Kannada Haridasa poets like Purandara Dasa used mythological references to develop themes of devotion and moral conduct.

- *Kazi Nazrul Islam* in Bengali literature used mythological allusions to agitate against colonial rule and promote revolution.

- *Subramania Bharati* in Tamil poetry drew upon themes from the Mahabharata and Ramayana to symbolize his vision of freedom and empowerment.

Role in Cultural and Social Contexts

1. Educational Tools:

Folk songs and poetry have traditionally served as educational tools, conveying moral and ethical lessons through the allegorical use of mythological symbols. The tales of virtue and vice help instill values in listeners, particularly in rural areas where storytelling is a primary form of entertainment and instruction.

2. Social Commentary:

Many folk poets have used mythological motifs to critique or reflect on contemporary social issues. Songs invoking gods like Vishnu or goddesses like Lakshmi often include pleas for intervention in times of social injustice or inequality, subtly referencing these deities' attributes of preservation and prosperity to comment on desired social reforms.

Adaptations and Relevance in Modern Media:

1.Modern Poetry and Literature:

Contemporary Indian poets and writers continue to draw on this rich symbolic repository. For example, Arundhati Roy's novel The God of Small Things uses mythological allegories to enhance themes of caste and gender discrimination. Such adaptations show the enduring ability of these symbols to convey complex ideas and emotions in a nuanced way.

2. Film and Television:

Indian cinema frequently incorporates mythological themes and characters, using them to comment on issues like corruption, crime, and moral decay. The use of these enduring symbols helps connect contemporary issues with ancient wisdom, making complex moral questions accessible and relatable to a wide audience.

Contemporary Relevance of Mythological Symbols:

1. Psychological Insight:

The characters from Indian mythology—through their triumphs, failures, virtues, and vices—offer profound insights into human psychology. Modern psychology and therapy sometimes use these stories and symbols to help individuals understand their own life stories and struggles, reflecting on characters like Arjuna's existential crisis in the Bhagavad Gita or Sita's trials in the Ramayana.

2.Moral and Ethical Reflection:

The moral dilemmas faced by characters in Indian mythology are emblematic of universal ethical questions. In today's world, where ethical ambiguities pervade public and private life, these stories offer a framework for reflecting on what it means to live a good life. They help individuals navigate the complexities of modern ethical decisions by providing examples of virtue, sacrifice, and compromise.

3. Unity in Diversity:

The vast array of deities and their diverse representations in Indian mythology symbolize the cultural and philosophical plurality of India. This diversity is particularly relevant in today's globalized world, promoting a message of tolerance and inclusiveness. By celebrating multiple paths to the divine, Indian mythology teaches respect for all beliefs and practices, fostering a sense of unity in diversity.

Broader Cultural Impact:

The use of mythological symbols in poetry and folk songs has had a profound impact on cultural identity and national consciousness in India. These artistic expressions help to keep the rich tapestry of Indian mythology alive, making it accessible to new generations and maintaining a sense of continuity with the past. They not only ensure that ancient wisdom is passed down but also allow for a reinterpretation of these myths in a modern context.

Examples in Global Literature:

Beyond Indian borders, the influence of these themes can be seen in global literature as well. Writers and poets from different cultures have drawn inspiration from Indian mythology, using similar motifs to explore universal themes. For instance, the idea of fate versus free will, a central theme in the story of Karna, is also a significant element in Western tragedies such as Shakespeare's Macbeth.

Educational and Psychological Use:

In educational settings, these mythological poems and stories serve as tools for teaching not only literature but also ethics and psychology. They provide rich material for discussion and analysis, helping students to develop critical thinking and emotional intelligence.In therapy, these myths are used to help clients explore personal issues through the lens of universal stories, offering insights into their own behaviors and choices. The symbolic nature of deities like Krishna or Durga can help individuals in therapy draw strength from these figures, using them as models for resilience and courage in their own lives.

Future Prospects:

As we look to the future, the role of these mythological symbols in literature and popular culture is likely to evolve but not diminish. The universal appeal of these stories ensures their place in the global narrative, while ongoing reinterpretations and adaptations will keep them relevant for new audiences. The continuing popularity of genres that blend traditional mythology with modern elements, such as fantasy and speculative fiction, suggests that the ancient gods and goddesses of India will continue to inspire and influence the world for generations to come.

By integrating these ancient myths with contemporary issues, writers and artists keep the dialogue between the past and the present alive, ensuring that the wisdom of the ages continues to enlighten the paths of individuals navigating the complexities of modern life. Through this ongoing cultural conversation, the mythological folk songs and poetry of India not only honor their roots but also sow seeds for future growth and understanding across the world.

Chapter 4: Historical and Archaeological Evidence - *DWARKA, AYODHYA, MAHABHARATA & THE RAM-SETU*

Exploration of archaeological findings supporting mythological events:

Indian mythology, particularly the epics of the Ramayana and the Mahabharata, has long been a subject of fascination and reverence for scholars, historians, and archaeologists alike. These texts not only offer rich narratives filled with complex characters and dramatic events but also provide a cultural and religious framework that has shaped Indian civilization for centuries. Over the years, several archaeological findings have been interpreted as potential evidence supporting the historical basis of some of these mythological events. This exploration delves into such findings, examining how they might correlate with the legendary tales recounted in Indian scriptures.

The Search for the Historical Krishna and Dwaraka:

One of the most significant focuses of archaeological study in relation to Indian mythology has been the ancient city of

Dwaraka, the kingdom ruled by Lord Krishna in the Mahabharata.

1. Underwater Explorations at Dwaraka:

Marine archaeology in the Gulf of Khambhat and the coastal town of Dwarka in Gujarat has yielded findings that some believe corroborate descriptions found in the Mahabharata. Excavations conducted by the Archaeological Survey of India (ASI) and other teams have discovered underwater structures, which are argued to be remnants of the ancient city submerged post-Krishna's era.

https://www.nodc.noaa.gov/archive/arc0001/9900162/2.2/data/0-data/jgofscd/htdocs/organisation/archaeology/Dwarka.htm (official Link)

Findings: Stone structures, pottery, and artifacts that could date back to the period described in the scriptures have been found beneath the water. These findings suggest that a historically significant city did exist in that region and might have been a thriving port.

2. Dating and Historical Analysis:

The challenge with correlating these findings with mythological narratives is the precise dating of the artifacts. Radiocarbon dating and other techniques have provided dates that are sometimes consistent with the timelines proposed for the Mahabharata events. However, definitive conclusions remain elusive due to the complex nature of the sedimentary layers and possible contamination over the ages.

The Ramayana and the Quest for Ayodhya:

The ancient city of Ayodhya, which is said to be the birthplace of Lord Rama, has also been the subject of archaeological scrutiny, particularly concerning the existence of temples at the disputed Ram Janmabhoomi site.

1. Excavations at Ayodhya:

Archaeological efforts have intensified in recent decades at Ayodhya. The ASI has conducted various digs at the site where the Babri Masjid once stood, and which Hindus revere as the birthplace of Rama.Findings: The ASI reports have indicated the presence of a temple under the mosque ruins, with the recovery of pillars, carvings, and other religious artifacts that suggest a pre-existing temple structure.

https://www.hindustantimes.com/india-news/remains-of-ancient-temple-discovered-at-ram-janmabhoomi-site-in-ups-ayodhya-says-trust-official-101694580472622-amp.html (official Link)

2. Historical Validity and Controversies:

The findings have been contentious and are subject to political and religious debates. Critics argue that the archaeological interpretations are influenced by contemporary socio-political agendas rather than unbiased scientific inquiry.

Ram Setu: The Adam's Bridge:

Another intriguing archaeological and geographical feature often linked to mythological narratives is the Ram Setu (also known as Adam's Bridge), a chain of limestone shoals between Pamban Island off the southeastern coast of Tamil Nadu, India, and Mannar Island off the northwestern coast of Sri Lanka.

1. Mythological Significance:

According to the Ramayana, this bridge was built by Lord Rama and his army of Vanaras (monkeys) to reach Lanka and rescue Sita from Ravana. It is described as being constructed from floating stones that were said to bear the name of Rama.

2. Scientific Investigations and Debates:

- **Satellite Imagery and Geological Studies:** Satellite imagery has shown a stretch of land submerged under shallow waters. This and geological studies suggest that this land connection between India and Sri Lanka may have existed until it was submerged under rising sea levels.

- **Archaeological Assessments:** Some studies suggest that some of the sandbanks are natural formations, while others propose that they could be ancient human or semi-human efforts to build a crossing. Critics of the theory argue that the shoals' formation is due to natural coral and sand accumulation, not human activity.

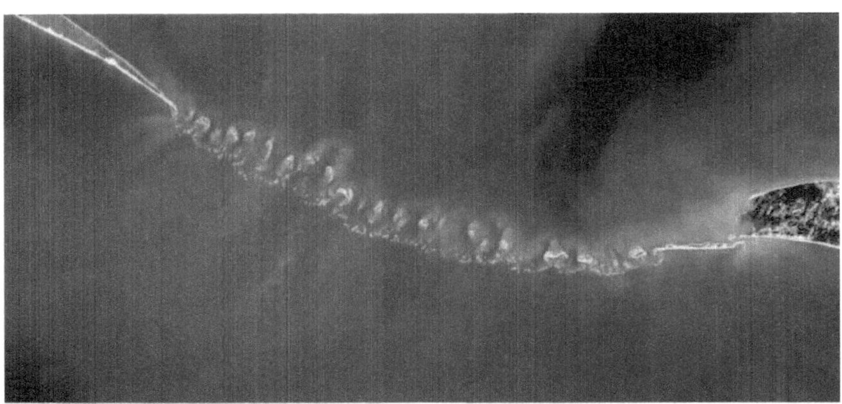

https://www.indiatoday.in/india/story/isro-to-ink-new-deal-to-identify-ram-setu-other-archeological-sites-2352230-2023-03-27 (official Link)

3. Cultural and Religious Relevance:

The existence of Ram Setu has a strong cultural and religious significance for many Hindus, who believe that the bridge's presence is direct physical evidence of the historical events described in the Ramayana. This site has become a pilgrimage destination for many, who view it as a tangible connection to the divine actions of Lord Rama.

Archaeo-astronomy and the Dating of the Mahabharata:

Archaeoastronomy has been used as a method to date the events of the Mahabharata by analyzing celestial references in the text and aligning them with astronomical data.

1. Planetary Positions:

Research into planetary positions described in the Mahabharata has been attempted to calculate the approximate time periods of the events narrated. For example, references to solar and lunar eclipses and the positions of planets like Jupiter and Saturn are used to create a timeline.

Findings: Some researchers have suggested dates around 3100 BCE as the time of the Mahabharata based on these alignments.

2. Criticism and Alternate Views:

Skeptics argue that the interpretations of celestial events in the texts are too vague and that the same configurations could repeat over centuries, making precise dating unreliable.

Implications for Historical and Cultural Studies:

The correlation between archaeological findings and mythological texts has significant implications for understanding the historical kernels of Indian mythology. These studies offer a fascinating glimpse into how ancient civilizations might have lived, celebrated, and constructed their societal norms around these epic tales.

1. Integrating Mythology with History:

These archaeological explorations help integrate mythological narratives with historical timelines, providing a more unified view of the past. They also help to validate the rich oral and written traditions of India as part of the country's historical legacy rather than merely as folklore.

2. Enhancing Cultural Identity:

For many in India, these findings enhance a sense of cultural identity and continuity. Discoveries like those at Dwaraka, Ayodhya, and Ram Setu link the present with the past, reinforcing traditional values and stories that have shaped Indian culture for millennia.

3. Promoting Interdisciplinary Research:

The quest to find historical bases for mythological events promotes interdisciplinary research involving archaeology, history, geology, and astronomy. This collaborative approach not only broadens the understanding of ancient texts but also enhances our knowledge of ancient Indian life and technologies.

While the potential connections between archaeological findings and mythological tales are compelling, they are not without controversy.

4.Technological Advances in Archaeology:

Advancements in technology, such as satellite imagery and enhanced carbon dating, have also played a crucial role in these Investigations. Example: The use of Ground Penetrating Radar (GPR) and other non-invasive technologies at sites like Ayodhya and Dwaraka have provided new layers of data and interpretations without the need for extensive excavations that could potentially damage these sensitive and sacred sites.

Conclusion:

The exploration of archaeological findings that might support the events described in Indian mythology provides a unique intersection of faith, science, and history. While definitive proof of many mythological events remains elusive, the ongoing research and debates they inspire are testament to the enduring power of these ancient stories. As excavations and studies continue, they not only help illuminate the past but also enrich our understanding of the ancient literature and civilizations that have shaped human history. Whether these findings prove the historical authenticity of mythological narratives or simply underscore their cultural importance, they contribute profoundly to our collective knowledge and appreciation of India's rich heritage.

xxx~¬~xxx

Historical records corroborating mythological narratives:

Indian mythology not only enchants with its rich tapestry of stories and characters but also provides a profound connection to India's historical and cultural fabric. Significant archaeological efforts have been directed towards exploring the truths behind the mythological narratives associated with Dwarka, Ayodhya, the Mahabharata, and Ram-Setu. These sites and stories offer a unique glimpse into the past, present, and future of India's cultural and historical landscape.

Dwarka: City of Lord Krishna:

Dwarka is described in ancient texts as a majestic city built by Lord Krishna that was later submerged under the sea. Modern-day Dwarka in Gujarat is associated with this mythological city.

- **Underwater Investigations:** Marine archaeologists have discovered evidence of ancient ruins submerged off the coast of present-day Dwarka. These include structures that some believe could have been part of a larger palatial complex, possibly the Dwarka mentioned in the texts.

- **Artifacts Found:** Items ranging from pottery, beads, sculptures, and pillars have been recovered, some dating back to 1500-2000 BCE, which support the existence of a thriving urban settlement that could correlate with descriptions from the scriptures.

Ayodhya: The Birthplace of Ram:

Ayodhya is revered as the birthplace of Lord Rama, central to the Hindu epic Ramayana, and has been a focal point of archaeological and socio-political interest.

- **Temple Evidence:** Excavations in the region have unearthed artifacts suggestive of ancient temples, including carvings and religious motifs that align with Hindu iconography.
- **Historical Continuity:** These findings help link the modern town with its ancient past, suggesting a continuous human settlement and

perhaps a cultural continuity from the era of the Ramayana.

Mahabharata: Epic of the Ages:

The Mahabharata's historical authenticity is explored through references to the Kurukshetra War and the extensive genealogies of characters that some historians believe align with archaeological findings.

- **Empirical Evidence:** Sites like Hastinapur have provided evidence of ancient settlements that show signs of catastrophic destruction and subsequent rebuilding, a narrative that fits descriptions in the Mahabharata.
- **Astronomical Software:** Modern software simulations of celestial

configurations described in the epic have been used to propose specific dates for events like the Kurukshetra War, suggesting a timeline that some scholars calculate to around 3100 BCE.

Ram-Setu: Bridge Between Nations:

Ram-Setu or Adam's Bridge, a chain of limestone shoals between India and Sri Lanka, is mythologically significant as it is said to have been built by Rama’s army.

- **Geological and Historical Analysis, Natural Formation Debate:** While geological studies suggest that the shoals are natural formations, others view them as corroborative evidence of the Ramayana’s narrative.

- **Strategic Importance:** The site has also been highlighted in contemporary discussions regarding its potential as a navigational channel, which would reshape the maritime boundaries and economic scenarios in the region.

Cultural and Political Impact: Cultural Heritage and Tourism:

- **Heritage Sites:** These archaeological sites attract millions of tourists both from within India and worldwide, helping to preserve and promote India's cultural heritage and mythology.

- **Educational Value:** These locations and their stories are used in educational curricula to teach history and cultural studies, providing a rich source of material that helps foster national identity and pride.

Political and Social Dimensions:

- **National Identity:** The exploration and preservation of these sites often feed into nationalistic narratives that are central to political discourse, particularly in India where history and religion are deeply intertwined with politics.

- **Religious Sentiments:** The sites like Ayodhya and Ram-Setu are emblematic of India's complex religious landscape, often being at the heart of socio-political debates and policies.

Looking to the Future:

The ongoing research and excavation in these mythologically significant areas continue to reveal new findings, each adding layers to our understanding of India's past. The blend of mythology, history, and science offers a unique narrative that is not only important for historical validation but also for its broader cultural, educational, and political implications.

Future Research and Preservation Efforts:

Academic and Scientific Studies

- **Advanced Technology:** Future archaeological efforts will likely integrate more advanced technology like satellite imagery, underwater archaeology tech, and carbon dating to provide clearer insights and more accurate datings of these ancient sites.

- **Interdisciplinary Approaches:** There is a growing trend towards interdisciplinary studies combining archaeology, history, geology, and even mythology to form a holistic view of the past. This approach allows for a more nuanced understanding of how these narratives and realities interweave.

Preservation and Conservation

- **UNESCO World Heritage Sites:** Efforts are being made to list sites such as Ayodhya and Dwarka under UNESCO's World Heritage Sites to ensure they are preserved for future generations. This not only helps protect these sites but also raises global awareness about their historical and cultural significance.

- **Local and Global Partnerships:** Collaborations between Indian and international archaeological teams can help boost the conservation efforts and bring in global best practices in site management and artifact preservation.

Cultural Impact and Educational Initiatives

- **National Curriculum:** There is a strong case for incorporating the historical aspects of these mythological narratives more prominently within the national educational curriculum. This would not only bolster national identity but also encourage a more informed understanding of India's rich historical tapestry among young students.

- **Museums and Exhibitions Interactive Displays:** Museums across India are beginning to feature more interactive and technologically advanced exhibitions that bring these ancient stories to life. Virtual reality setups, holographic displays, and interactive timelines could significantly enhance visitors' experiences and educational value.

- **Traveling Exhibits:** To reach a broader audience, traveling exhibits about these mythological and historical sites can be organized globally, showcasing the rich cultural heritage of India and educating the world about its ancient civilizations.

Political and Social Narrative

1. **Cultural Diplomacy:**

- **Global Forums:** India can use its rich mythological and historical heritage as a tool for cultural diplomacy, engaging with global audiences and forming cultural ties based on shared heritage and interests in human history.

- **Tourism and Soft Power:** By promoting these sites internationally, India can enhance its soft power globally, attracting tourists, scholars, and historians to explore the deep-rooted cultural narratives and archaeological wonders of the country.

2. Religious Harmony:

- **Interfaith Dialogues:** The historical and archaeological exploration of these sites also provides an opportunity for interfaith dialogue by highlighting the multi-layered narratives and the pluralistic past of India. This can help mitigate religious conflicts and promote harmony.

- **Community Involvement:** Ensuring that local communities are involved in and benefit from the archaeological explorations and tourism can help promote communal harmony and collective pride in their regional history.

Conclusion:

The quest to intertwine the strands of mythology, history, and archaeology concerning sites like Dwarka, Ayodhya, Mahabharata, and Ram-Setu not only enriches our understanding of India's past but also reinforces the cultural continuity that has been central to Indian identity. As these explorations yield more insights and as modern science sheds new light on old tales, the stories of gods and warriors will continue to hold a mirror to the beliefs, values, and aspirations of the civilization that treasured them. In this way, the past, present, and future of Indian mythology and history remain inextricably linked, continually influencing and inspiring generations across the globe.

xxx~x~¬~xxx~¬~xxx~¬~xxx~xxx

Chapter 5: Scientific Interpretations

Examination of scientific theories aligning with mythological accounts:

Indian mythology is replete with fantastical elements that have fascinated readers and scholars for centuries. From flying chariots and potent herbs to conversations with extraterrestrial beings and divine weapons, these elements, while often regarded as purely symbolic or allegorical, have also been explored through the lens of modern science to understand their potential basis in reality. Here, we delve into how contemporary scientific theories and advancements might align with, or explain, some of the most intriguing mythological accounts.

Pushpak Vimana: Ancient Flying Machines:

The concept of the Pushpak Vimana, often described in texts like the Ramayana as a flying chariot or aircraft used by the gods, is one of the most captivating technological wonders mentioned in ancient Indian scriptures.

Scientific Theories and Explorations

- **Ancient Aviation:** Some proponents of ancient astronaut theories and ancient technologies argue that descriptions of the Vimanas could be grounded in a reality of advanced engineering knowledge that may have existed in ancient times and subsequently been lost to history.

- **Aeronautical Science:** Modern aeronautical research has occasionally looked to descriptions of Vimanas for inspiration, considering whether they might metaphorically represent sophisticated understanding of aerodynamics by ancient scholars.

Sanjeevani Booti: The Life-Restoring Herb:

Sanjeevani Booti, a herb mentioned in the Ramayana, was said to have the power to revive the lifeless. Lord Hanuman is famously recounted to have transported this herb to heal Lakshmana.

Botanical Studies and Theories

- **Search for the Herb:** Botanists and researchers have speculated about historical and ayurvedic texts to identify this mythical herb with plants having known medicinal properties. Although no exact match has been found, some hypothesize that it refers to a group of high-altitude plants that have exceptional regenerative and healing properties.

- **Medicinal Plants Research:** Ongoing research into Himalayan flora often looks to align ancient descriptions with contemporary findings, suggesting that Sanjeevani might symbolize the broader healing capabilities of certain botanical species.

Ravana's Lal Kitab or Red Book:

Ravana's Lal Kitab, often thought to contain dark arts and secrets of astrology and mysticism, holds a significant place in mythological lore.

Cultural and Astrological Study

- **Astrological Manuals:**

  The Lal Kitab is a set of five Sanskrit language books on Hindu astrology and palmistry, written in the 19th century, which many believe were inspired by ancient texts possibly linked to mythological figures like Ravana. Researchers study these texts to unravel astrological beliefs embedded within cultural narratives.

Conversations with Aliens and Otherworldly Beings:

Ancient texts occasionally describe interactions with beings from other worlds, which some interpret as early accounts of alien contact.

Extraterrestrial Hypotheses:

- **Ancient Astronaut Theories:**

  These interactions have been examined under theories suggesting that ancient civilizations might have been visited by alien species. Artifacts such as the depiction of flying machines or Vimanas are sometimes cited as evidence in these discussions.

Brahmastra and Other Divine Weapons:

The Brahmastra, described in various texts as a weapon of mass destruction, capable of annihilating entire legions, could be paralleled with modern nuclear weapons.

Theoretical Physics and Weaponry

- **Energy Weapons Concept:** Some researchers have drawn parallels between descriptions of the Brahmastra and modern theories of energy weapons or nuclear capabilities, speculating that ancient myths might metaphorically describe advanced scientific knowledge.

Healing Abilities and Mutant Powers:

The myriad healing abilities and powers described in Indian mythology, such as those possessed by gods and powerful sages, have fascinated geneticists and medical researchers.

Genetic and Biomedical Correlations

- **Genetic Engineering:** Advances in genetic modification and biomedical sciences provide a modern context in which to re-examine these mythological abilities. For example, the concept of someone healing rapidly from wounds may today be discussed in terms of accelerated cellular regeneration technologies.

Conclusion:

While it is crucial to approach these subjects with a scientific skepticism, the exploration of mythological narratives through the lens of modern science provides a fascinating intersection between the ancient and the contemporary. Whether these stories are metaphors for natural phenomena, lost knowledge, or simply creative fiction, they continue to inspire scientific curiosity and cultural pride. The melding of past lore with current scientific inquiry not only enriches our understanding of these myths but also underscores the timeless urge to explore and rationalize the world around us.

xxx~¬~xxx

Examples of how modern science explains mythical phenomena:

Indian mythology is rich with characters who possess mystical powers and abilities that defy the conventional laws of nature. These tales, which feature events and powers such as teleportation, invincibility, and omniscience, offer fertile ground for comparison with modern scientific theories, particularly those involving concepts like the multiverse and parallel universes.

Mystical Powers and Modern Science:

The astounding powers depicted in Indian mythology might be viewed through the lens of contemporary scientific paradigms to explore possible explanations or analogies in modern physics and other sciences.

- **Teleportation and Quantum Mechanics**

  - **Quantum Teleportation:** Modern advancements in quantum mechanics and the phenomenon of quantum entanglement, where particles remain connected no matter how far apart they are, could be likened to the teleportation abilities described in mythological texts. For instance, the ability of sages to appear and disappear at will echoes the quantum teleportation experiments being explored today.

- **Invincibility and Material Science**

  - **Metamaterials:** The concept of invincibility, such as that possessed by characters who are immune to conventional weapons, can be correlated with research into metamaterials. These are composite materials designed to have properties not found in naturally occurring materials, potentially used to develop real-life invisibility cloaks or shields that divert attacks.

- **Omniscience and Artificial Intelligence**

  - **AI and Predictive Analytics:** The power of omniscience, or all-knowing intelligence, mirrors contemporary developments in artificial intelligence, where machines can predict outcomes based on vast data analysis. This technological parallel offers a modern counterpart to the mythological narratives of seers and prophets.

Multiverse and Parallel Universe Theories:

The concepts of multiverse and parallel universes provide another intriguing framework for interpreting the diverse and fantastical elements of Indian mythology.

- **Multiverse Theory**
  - **Multiple Realities:** Modern physics contemplates the

possibility of multiple universes existing simultaneously, each having different versions of reality. This could provide a scientific backdrop to mythological stories where multiple realms exist, such as the heavenly planets and the underworld, each with its own set of inhabitants and laws of physics.

- **Parallel Universes**
  - **Alternative Scenarios:** The idea that parallel universes might coexist with our own universe can be seen in stories where gods intervene in human affairs; different outcomes of the same event are explored, reflecting the complex narrative structures similar to the hypothetical scenarios in parallel universe theories.

Application in Modern Narratives and Theories

❖ Cultural Impact and Contemporary Fiction

- **Science Fiction:** These mythological themes have heavily influenced modern science fiction literature and media, where concepts such as time travel, alternate realities, and advanced technologies form the core of many popular stories.

- **Philosophical Implications:** The parallels between ancient mythological concepts and modern scientific theories also enrich philosophical inquiries into the nature of reality, existence, and consciousness.

❖ Theoretical Physics and Cosmology

➢ Cosmological Speculations:

Discussions about the structure of the universe in Indian texts often include multiple layers or dimensions, which can be speculative analogs to scientific models in cosmology dealing with multiple dimensions in space-time proposed in theories like string theory.

Educational and Research Perspectives

❖ Interdisciplinary Studies

- **Academic Curricula:** Integrating discussions about mythology with scientific theories in academic curricula could promote interdisciplinary learning and stimulate interest in both fields.
- **Research Dialogues:** Encouraging dialogues between mythology scholars and scientists could lead to new insights and interpretations that bridge the gap between these traditionally separate disciplines.

Conclusion:

The exploration of mystical powers and mythological narratives through the lens of modern science, particularly concepts like multiverse and parallel universes, not only highlights the timeless appeal of these stories but also encourages a deeper understanding of both ancient wisdom and contemporary scientific achievements. By examining these parallels, we can appreciate how mythological imaginations might have been ancient interpretations of ideas that science is only now beginning to explore. This synthesis of mythology and science enriches our cultural heritage and scientific knowledge, fostering a holistic view of human inquiry and imagination.

Chapter 6: Controversies and Debates

Addressing Controversies Surrounding Interpretations of Indian Mythology: A Detailed Debate

Indian mythology, particularly the epics of the Mahabharata and the Ramayana, is rich in narratives that have shaped the cultural and spiritual landscape of India for centuries. However, the interpretation of these texts is often subject to significant controversy, both within scholarly circles and in the public domain. This discourse examines various controversies surrounding the interpretations of Indian mythology, discussing archaeological, linguistic, philosophical, and scientific perspectives to provide a well-rounded debate on the subject.

Historical Validity vs. Mythological Narrative:

One of the primary controversies in the interpretation of Indian mythology revolves around the historical validity of the events described in these texts.

- **Archaeological Evidence**

  a. **Supporting Evidence:** Excavations in areas like Hastinapur, Kurukshetra, and

Ayodhya have unearthed artifacts that some claim corroborate the narratives found in the epics. For instance, the Archaeological Survey of India (ASI) has reported findings of chariot parts and weapons in Kurukshetra that date back to around the time the Mahabharata is supposed to have occurred.

b. **Skeptical Viewpoints:** Critics argue that such findings, while suggestive, do not conclusively prove that the events of the epics happened as described. They caution against reading these as direct evidence of the mythological narratives, suggesting instead that these could be coincidental or misinterpreted.

- **Linguistic Studies**

    a. **Philological Analysis:** Researchers analyzing the language and composition of the Vedas, Ramayana, and Mahabharata suggest that these texts underwent numerous revisions and compilations over centuries. This suggests a blend of historical core events with added mythological elements.

    b. **Counterpoint:** Traditionalists often argue that changes in the text do not dilute their historical core and that the essence of the narratives points to a truth about ancient Indian civilization and its values.

The Role of Astronomy and Cosmology:

Another significant area of debate is the astronomical references in these texts, which some claim date the events precisely.

Astronomical Alignments

- **Support:** Researchers like Dr. B. N. Narahari Achar and Dr. P. V. Vartak have used planetary software to match descriptions of celestial configurations in texts to argue for specific dates for events like the Mahabharata war.

- **Criticism:** Critics argue that these interpretations are often forced and rely on selective reading of texts. They also point out that astronomical configurations recur cyclically, making precise dating unreliable.

Philosophical and Ethical Interpretations:

The philosophical and ethical teachings of the epics, particularly the Bhagavad Gita, are often cited as evidence of the texts' profound moral underpinnings and historical importance.

Philosophical Depth

- **In Favor:** Proponents argue that the sophisticated philosophical discourse in the Gita, concerning duty (dharma), righteousness, and the path to liberation (moksha), reflects an advanced ancient culture and suggests a historical context where such ideas were discussed and valued.

- **Opposing Views:** Skeptics might concede the philosophical depth but argue that this does not necessarily corroborate the historical accuracy of the narrative events in the Gita or the Mahabharata.

Genetic and Anthropological Studies:

Recent advances in genetic and anthropological studies have also entered the debate regarding the origins and histories described in Indian mythology.

Genetic Research

- **Supporting Data:** Studies of Indian population genetics have shown some consistencies with the migrations and gene flows described in texts like the Rig Veda, suggesting that there might be a kernel of historical truth in these accounts.
- **Criticism:** Opponents argue that genetic data is too broad to be directly linked to narratives and should be interpreted with caution.

Cultural and Social Impact:

The interpretation of mythology also has profound implications for Indian society and culture, influencing education, politics, and social norms.

Cultural Identity

- **Support:** For many, these texts and their interpretations are a source of cultural pride and identity, offering a sense of continuity with India's ancient past.
- **Concerns:** There is concern that nationalistic interpretations can lead to exclusionary or biased histories that may marginalize minority groups and perspectives.

The Ten Avatars of Vishnu and Their Symbolic Representation of Human Evolution:

The mythological narrative of human evolution in Hindu tradition is beautifully encapsulated through the Dashavatara, which are the ten incarnations of Lord Vishnu. According to Hindu mythology, Vishnu, one of the principal deities of the trinity (Trimurti) that includes Brahma and Shiva, descends to Earth in various forms or avatars to restore cosmic order and protect dharma (righteousness or moral order) against adharma (the force of evil). These avatars of Vishnu are symbolic of different stages of cosmic evolution, from the simplest life forms to more complex beings, reflecting a divine response to the evolving needs of the world.

Contemporary Interpretation and Relevance

These avatars not only depict the evolution from aquatic forms to fully rational humans but also encapsulate the evolution of human society and its moral and ethical framework. The philosophical underpinnings of the Dashavatara have resonated deeply with evolutionary biology, and some scholars have found intriguing parallels between Darwinian theory and Vishnu's incarnations, although such comparisons are generally symbolic rather than scientific.

The Dashavatara serves as a profound narrative framework that provides insights into Hindu cosmological and philosophical thought, emphasizing the cyclical nature of time and the continuous presence of the divine in guiding and shaping human destiny. Each incarnation of Vishnu addresses a particular aspect of existence and morality, reflecting the eternal and omnipresent nature of Vishnu, adapting to the needs of the cosmos in various forms.

This mythological view of evolution is not only a reflection of Hindu theological and cosmological thinking but also a cultural narrative that has guided countless generations through the moral and spiritual landscapes of life.

Cultural and Philosophical Dimensions of the Dashavatara

The Dashavatara does more than just chart a course of biological or physical evolution; it delves into the psychological, spiritual, and ethical progression of humanity. Each avatar of Vishnu not only adapts to the needs of the world at a specific time but also addresses the evolving spiritual and moral questions faced by humanity.

Integration with Vedic and Upanishadic Philosophy

The avatars often embody concepts found in the Vedas and Upanishads. For example, the Narasimha avatar, emerging from a pillar, underscores the Upanishadic teaching that the divine essence (Brahman) is in everything. This avatar, which transcends simple categorization as either man or animal, inside or outside, day or night, illustrates the profound concept of the omnipresence of the divine and the limitations of human understanding.

Ram and Dharm

Rama's adherence to dharma, even in the face of personal loss and suffering, provides an enduring lesson on duty, righteousness, and moral integrity. His life teaches the importance of following one's ethical duties, which has had a profound impact on Indian society, influencing legal and social norms. Rama's character has been idealized in various cultural expressions and is often considered the epitome of virtue.

Krishna and Bhakti

Krishna introduces a shift from the adherence to ritualistic dharma to a more personal relationship with the divine through devotion (bhakti). His teachings in the Bhagavad Gita, advocating for a selfless, dedicated action without attachment to results, have influenced various schools of Indian philosophy and spirituality. The Gita's dialogues during the Mahabharata war emphasize human agency, the nature of life and death, and the importance of duty (Karma Yoga), knowledge (Jnana Yoga), and devotion (Bhakti Yoga).

Buddha and the Path to Enlightenment

The inclusion of Buddha as an avatar of Vishnu illustrates the assimilative nature of Hindu theology, embracing Buddha's teachings on suffering, detachment, and compassion, and interpreting them within the broader Hindu cosmos. This reflects a significant cultural synthesis and highlights the adaptability of Hindu philosophy to encompass divergent viewpoints and integrate them into a cohesive religious framework.

Kalki and the Concept of Renewal

The prophesied avatar of Kalki, expected to appear at the end of the Kali Yuga, the current age of decline, resonates with the universal mythic theme of apocalypse and renewal. This avatar's role is to eradicate evil and restore dharma, leading to the renewal of the cosmos. This belief instills hope and the expectation of moral and cosmic rectification, reinforcing the cyclic nature of time and existence in Hindu thought.

Modern Relevance and Global Impact

The narratives of the Dashavatara continue to be relevant in contemporary discussions of ethics, governance, environmentalism, and human rights. Each avatar's story can be seen as a case study in handling the complex challenges that arise at different stages of societal development and personal growth.

- **Environmentalism and Varaha:** The story of Varaha can be interpreted as a divine intervention to save the earth from destruction, a narrative that resonates with modern efforts to address environmental degradation.

- **Leadership and Rama:** Rama's principled rule is often cited in leadership seminars and ethical discussions as an ideal for leaders in both political and corporate spheres.

- **Personal Development and Krishna:** Krishna's diverse roles as a playful child, a lover, a kingmaker, and a philosopher attract people from various walks of life, offering lessons on handling life's various roles with grace and dignity.

- In concluding it, The Dashavatara not only provides a mythological schema of the evolution of life and the universe but also offers profound insights into the human condition, exploring themes of morality, leadership, duty, and spirituality. This deep reservoir of mythological content serves as a cultural and spiritual guide for individuals and societies, helping to navigate the moral landscapes of modern life. In a world grappling with rapid change and ethical dilemmas, the timeless lessons of the Dashavatara provide not only a link to India's ancient past but also a beacon for the future, demonstrating the enduring power and relevance of these mythological narratives.

Conclusion:

The interpretation of Indian mythology is a complex and multifaceted issue, encompassing debates over archaeological, linguistic, philosophical, and scientific data. While there is evidence that suggests some aspects of these mythologies might have historical bases, conclusive proofs are elusive, and interpretations often reflect broader cultural, political, and social biases. As scholarship advances and new technologies emerge, the debate over these ancient narratives will likely continue to evolve, reflecting the deep and enduring impact these stories have on Indian and global culture. This ongoing dialogue not only enriches our understanding of the past but also informs contemporary discussions about morality, identity, and the human condition.

The Conclusion: Reflection on the enduring relevance of Indian mythology:

Reflecting on the profound discourse surrounding Indian mythology, particularly in the context of its interpretations and the controversies it engenders, it becomes evident that these ancient narratives are far more than just stories passed down through generations. They are, indeed, a vibrant tapestry of cultural, philosophical, and moral reflections that continue to resonate deeply within the collective consciousness of modern India, particularly within Hindu ideology. In considering their ongoing relevance, one must appreciate the nuanced interplay of history, religion, and nationalism that these texts inspire in contemporary society.

At the heart of this discourse lies the undeniable fact that Indian mythology—embodied primarily by the epics of the Ramayana and the Mahabharata—has not only survived the relentless test of time but has thrived, influencing countless aspects of daily life, politics, education, and social norms in India.

It is both amusing and awe-inspiring that narratives conceived thousands of years ago still manage to hold the rapt attention of scholars and laymen alike, fueling debates that reach into the very core of national identity and historical authenticity.

Cultural and National Pride

The Ramayana and the Mahabharata, with their intricate depictions of dharma (duty/righteousness), artha (purpose), kama (desire), and moksha (liberation), offer more than just moral guidance; they provide a lens through which the past converses with the present. The pride with which these texts are upheld by proponents of Hindu ideology is not merely about cultural nostalgia but about celebrating a heritage perceived as superior in its moral and philosophical depth. How delightful it is that modern India, with all its technological advancements and its ambitions of space exploration and digital revolutions, still finds time to debate the nuances of ancient mythological weapons and divine interventions! It's as if Oppenheimer himself quoted the Bhagavad Gita out of sheer reverence—or was it a warning?

Education and Integration into Mainstream Discourse

In educational settings, Indian mythology is not just a subject of historical study but serves as a vibrant resource to engage students with ethical dilemmas, governance, environmental stewardship, and the complexities of human relationships.

Texts like the Bhagavad Gita are dissected in management schools, and the strategies used in the Mahabharata are studied in military academies. What a sophisticated way to integrate thousands of years old "myths" into cutting-edge curricula, ensuring that Arjuna's existential crisis and Krishna's counsel are as debated as global economic policies and theories of leadership.

Political Machinations and Social Harmony

The political leverage that these epics provide is not lost on anyone, least of all the political strategists who align themselves with Hindu ideology. The construction of temples, the organized celebrations of Hindu festivals, and the evocative recounting of these epics at political rallies are not just acts of devotion but calculated moves in the grand chessboard of Indian politics. It is both ironic and spectacular how ancient myths are employed to forge modern political identities and national unity. It's almost as if Hanuman is leaping across political constituencies with Sanjeevani herbs to heal the wounds of division!

Global Influence and Diaspora

On the global stage, Indian mythology has transcended geographical boundaries, influencing international cinema, literature, and art. The diaspora carries these stories in their hearts, often using them to connect with their cultural roots and share their rich heritage with the world. Festivals like Diwali and Holi, celebrated with gusto across continents, are testament to the universal appeal and enduring charm of these narratives. Oh, how the world loves the spectacle of color, light, and moral righteousness served with an exotic side of curry!

Conclusion

In sum, the enduring relevance of Indian mythology, particularly within Hindu ideology, is a phenomenon to behold. In an age dominated by digital media and artificial intelligence, the fact that discussions about ancient mythological texts can still stir national debate and inspire cultural festivals is a delicious paradox. It highlights a collective yearning for identity and continuity amidst rapid modernization and change. Indian mythology, thus, serves not just as a relic of the past but as a living, breathing aspect of contemporary Indian identity that is both gloriously proud and subtly ironic in its persistence. How remarkable it is that a nation poised on the edge of future technological revolutions still looks back at its mythological past not just for lessons but for a sense of pride and belonging. Truly, mythology is not just mythology; it is the very soul of India, narrating its past, shaping its present, and potentially guiding its future.

Thank You Note

Dear Readers,

Thank you for choosing to embark on this enlightening journey with "Indian Mythology: Fiction Becoming Facts." Your interest and support mean the world to me and fuel my passion for uncovering the truths hidden within ancient myths.

Each page you've turned has not only deepened our collective understanding but also connected us through the timeless stories of Indian mythology. I am deeply grateful for your curiosity and engagement, which inspire lively debates and a shared exploration of our world's rich cultural heritage.

Thank you for being part of this adventure. Your enthusiasm and thoughtful reflections encourage me to continue this quest for knowledge and truth. I hope this book has provided you with valuable insights and a fresh perspective on the myths that have shaped civilizations across time.

Warmest regards,

Prakhar Mishra

www.ingramcontent.com/pod-product-compliance
Lightning Source LLC
Chambersburg PA
CBHW051152130726
47988CB00005B/2092

* 9 7 9 8 8 9 3 6 3 5 3 7 9 *